IN THE FOOTSTEPS OF

THOMAS & EMMA HARDY

An account of their time in Cornwall

By Heulyn & Ginny Lewis

3rd Edition 2015

ISBN 978-0-9572340-1-7

Thomas Hardy
(1840 - 1928)

Aged 29 in March 1870, on first impression he seemed older than he was, with a yellowish beard and shabby great coat, presenting quite a *"business appearance"*. He was shy, callow, bookish and spoke softly.
In his autobiography, he describes his immaturity at the time as *".. greater than is common for his years, and it may be mentioned here that a clue to much of his character and action throughout his life is afforded by his lateness of development in virility, while mentally precocious."*

Emma Lavinia Gifford
(1840 - 1912)

Though her features were not regular, her complexion was flawless, her deep grey eyes showed vitality and her corn-coloured hair worn in long ringlets, gave her *"the look of the old pictures in Hampton Court Palace"*. Her figure and movement was graceful and her manner was vivacious, displaying a fresh naturalness. In her speech she expressed a directness, which could be as charming and admirable as it could be tactless and disconcerting. At the age of 29, in March 1870, Emma made a striking figure.

▲
Boscastle Harbour
painted by William
Gibbons (1841-1886)
in 1875

IN THE FOOTSTEPS OF

THOMAS & EMMA HARDY

Although Thomas and Emma Hardy both contributed briefly to Boscastle and the area in their own ways, particularly with the restoration of St Juliot Church, the effect of this part of Cornwall on their lives, was far more influential. This remote piece of rugged land, farmed and cared for by successive generations, altered both their lives and consequently the course of English literature.

In the words of Emma Hardy, some 40 years after leaving the area... *"Scarcely any author and his wife could have had a much more romantic meeting"* adding... *"this very remote spot, with beautiful sea-coast, and the wild Atlantic ocean rolling in with its magnificent waves and spray."* The landscape continues to captivate, with its unique, primal qualities, unleashing the *"power to awaken heart and soul."*

THOMAS HARDY

Thomas Hardy was born in the hamlet of Higher Bockhampton, near Dorchester, in 1840. His father and grandfather were successful builders by trade. His mother, Jemima, read widely and passed on her passion for books to her first-born, Thomas. He was a frail child, who learnt to read at an early age, but did not start attending the local school until he was eight years old.

In 1850 he was thought fit enough to walk the three miles to Dorchester each day to Last's School, where he was a keen pupil, taking Latin as an extra subject.

Thomas Hardy, aged 16, 1856 ▼

At the age of 16, Thomas was noticed by the respected Dorchester architect John Hicks, who offered him an apprenticeship. For the next few years he continued his daily walks to and from the town, often reading for several hours before setting off to work and teaching himself Greek in the evenings. Hicks was a good employer and encouraged Hardy's interest in the Classics.

In 1862, Hardy left for London where he was soon employed by architect, Arthur Blomfield, in a large and fashionable practice on the Thames. Whilst Hardy did not make many friends in the capital he made the most of its cultural opportunities by going to concerts, dances and galleries. He continued to read vast amounts of poetry and wrote many verses, all of which were rejected by publishers. However, a paper written for his fellow architects called *How I Built*

Myself a House was printed and this small success encouraged Hardy to concentrate on prose. His first book *The Poor Man and the Lady* was completed in 1868. This also was rejected for publication, but the reviewers advised the young author to concentrate on his strengths i.e. portraying rural scenes and characters in a novel with a strong plot. With this in mind Hardy began to write *Desperate Remedies*, which was to become his first published novel.

Five years of unrelenting study and city living began to take its toll on Hardy's health. In mid 1867 he returned to Dorset and resumed working for Hicks. When Hicks died in 1869 his practice was taken over by G.R. Crickmay who gave Hardy the task of overseeing church restorations.

Weymouth,
11th February, 1870.

Dear Sir:
Can you go into Cornwall for me, to take a plan and particulars of a church I am about to rebuild there? It must be done early next week, and I should be glad to see you on the Monday morning. Yours truly,
G.R. Crickmay

In 1870, Hardy was assigned to visit St Juliot on the remote north coast of Cornwall and survey the church there. He was reluctant to go. His first novel, *Desperate Remedies*, was almost completed and he did not welcome the distraction. Eventually, however, he was persuaded to take on the project, little knowing that this visit would shape the rest of his life.

On Monday the 7th of March he rose at 4am and commenced his starlit walk to Dorchester station where he boarded a train to Cornwall. After an arduous twelve hour trip he arrived at Launceston, climbed the hill to the town for refreshment, then hired a pony and trap for the next stage of his journey; across the romantic expanse of Bodmin Moor, to St Juliot.

Thomas Hardy, aged 29, 1870 ▼

It was shortly after dark when he arrived at St Juliot's Rectory. He was welcomed at the porch by a woman who introduced herself as Emma Lavinia Gifford, sister-in-law to the Rev. Caddell Holder, who was in bed suffering from gout.

Hardy's first impression of Emma was noted in matter-of-fact style in his diary entry for that evening... *"Received by young lady in brown,"* which shows nothing of the instant infatuation written about when he reminisced in old age...

"And so I never once guessed / A Love-nest, / Bowered and candle-lit, lay / In my way, / Till I found a hid hollow, / Where I burst on her my heart could not but follow."

(The Discovery)

Emma's recollection of the event was more emotional... *"I was immediately arrested by his familiar appearance, as if I had seen him in a dream."* Indeed, Emma thought quite literally that Thomas was the 'man of her dreams' and that the two had been destined to meet from birth, with fate conspiring to bring them together. Hardy on the other hand saw the meeting as purely accidental - a product of chance happenings.

On that first night, although he must have been tired, Hardy went to the parlour after the evening meal to talk and play music with Emma and her sister Helen Holder. The hours spent by candle-light, being entertained at the piano during that first visit must have made a deep impression on Hardy as he wrote of it later in many poems. A mutual liking for music would have added to the attraction that Hardy and Emma began to feel for each other...

▲ Porch of St Juliot's Old Rectory

"A woman was playing, / A man looking on; / And the mould of her face, / And her neck, and her hair, / Which the rays fell upon / Of the two candles there, / Sent him mentally straying / In some fancy-place / Where pain had no trace."

(At the Piano)

Hardy's second day at St Juliot was spent at the church, drawing plans and measuring up. It seems that most of his work was completed by that evening, but he decided to prolong his visit until the end of the week.

On Wednesday, March 9th, Hardy accompanied Mrs Holder and Emma on a tour of Boscastle, Tintagel and Penpethy slate quarries *"with a view to the church roofing"*. The following day, he and Emma were bold enough to spend the morning on the cliffs unchaperoned. She rode her mare and Hardy walked alongside...

"The pale mews plained below us, and the waves seemed far away / In a nether sky, engrossed in saying their ceaseless babbling say, / As we laughed light-heartedly aloft on that clear-sunned March day."

(Beeny Cliff)

At dawn on Friday, March 11th, Hardy bid adieu to Emma and the poem *At the Word "Farewell"*, suggests that they may have parted with a kiss...

"- But crimson one cheek of hers burned / When we came in together."

There is little doubt that the pair were in love by the end of this first brief visit to the Rectory in 1870.

▲ Hardy's sketch of bench ends at St Juliot Church, 1870

Hardy's next visit to Emma at St Juliot was in August that same year. This time they had longer to get acquainted and Emma showed Hardy more of the area that she loved. On their frequent trips out they went to Tintagel with its romantic ruined castle, to Trebarwith Strand, to Bossiney, past the Strangles to Bude and to other places along the coast. At other times, they went alone, riding the cliff-tops, or walking down to Boscastle through the leafy Valency Valley.

On Sunday, August 14th, the couple walked across to Lesnewth for Evensong by candlelight. The churchwarden was Henry Jose, a 25 year old farmer who was an admirer of Emma, no doubt favouring her fresh and vivacious nature in the same way Hardy did. She was obviously attracted towards the young local man, describing him in her *Recollections* as *"...a man gentle of nature, musical, christlike in guilelessness, handsome of face and figure..."*

Since Emma was approaching 30 and living in a place with few opportunities to meet suitable 'husband material', Jose may well have succeeded in his ambition to marry Miss Gifford had not Hardy turned up on the scene. In *The Young Churchwarden*, Hardy describes the moment when Jose sees him and Emma sitting together in the service *"...he scanned / Her and me, his vanquished air / Hinted that his dream was done..."*

▲ The Rev. Caddell Holder, Emma (standing) & her sister Helen. The Rectory, August 1870

On these daily summer outings the two sketched and talked of books, Emma was fascinated by her intellectual suitor and their conversations must have reminded her of the lively social scene she had previously enjoyed during her upbringing in Plymouth.

"We grew much interested in each other...he was quite unlike any other person who came to see us, for they were slow of speech and ideas..."

Emma also had aspirations as a writer and encouraged Hardy from the start to pursue his literary talents, giving him the confidence to choose writing over a career in architecture. She also helped him practically, by making copies of his manuscripts for publishers, doing research and suggesting alterations. The fact that her assistance was not given the recognition she felt it deserved caused jealously and resentment in later years.

River Valency

But back in that happy August week in 1870, one day in particular seems to have made a life-long impression.

On Friday the 19th, they walked again alongside the Valency and had a picnic by a small waterfall. Here they lost a glass in the cool stream and, forty years on, they both remembered the event. Emma in her *Recollections* says... *"We had to jump over stones and climb over a low wall by rough steps, get through by narrow pathways to come out on great wide spaces suddenly, with a sparkling little brook going the same way, into which we once lost a tiny picnic-tumbler, and there it is to this day no doubt between two small boulders..."*

Hardy wrote, using Emma's viewpoint...

"I held the vessel to rinse in the fall, / Where it slipped, and sank, and was past recall, / Though we stooped and plumbed the little abyss / With long bared arms. There the glass still is."

He sketched Emma at the time, reaching into the pool with the sleeves of her dress rolled up.

"No lip has touched it since his and mine / In turns from there sipped lovers' wine."

(Under the Waterfall)

Today the scene is so unchanged from the time of their visit that it is tempting to imagine the tumbler, still lodged in a crevice, under the water-polished stones.

On his return to Dorset, Hardy eventually succeeded in getting his novel *Desperate Remedies* published, largely at his own expense. It was met with mixed reviews, but served to introduce Hardy to the literary world and to the educated public.

Spurred on by this he speedily wrote *Under the Greenwood Tree*, re-using some material from *The Poor Man and the Lady* (which he later destroyed). When the manuscript was not enthusiastically received by Macmillan the publishers Hardy became disillusioned with writing and returned to London and architecture. The book was eventually published and although well reviewed it was not a great public success.

▲ Hardy's sketch entitled *Searching for the glass*, dated August 19, 1870

Hardy next visited St Juliot briefly in May, and again (unannounced) for a longer stay in October 1871. In *The Face at the Casement*, he recalls an evening trip with Emma to the vicarage at St Clether. The reason for the visit was to enquire about the health of the Curate's ailing son, another of Emma's admirers.

Kirland House ▼

Almost a year passed before Hardy returned to Cornwall. To help ease the pain of these long separations Emma had given Hardy a lock of her hair as a keepsake - rediscovered and recalled by him after her death in 1912.

"When your soft welcomings were said, / This curl was waving on your head, / And when we walked where breakers dinned / It sported in the sun and wind, / And when I had won your words of grace / It brushed and clung about my face. / Then, to abate the misery / Of absentness, you gave it me."
(On a Discovered Curl of Hair)

This poem also hints at the reason for Hardy's August visit in 1872 i.e. to be introduced to the Gifford family, to whom he planned to announce his intention to marry Emma.

The Gifford home at that time was Kirland House, on the outskirts of Bodmin (Rou'tor Town). It is thought that Hardy may have stayed here for a while, even after being dismissed as an unworthy suitor by Emma's disagreeable and snobbish father, John Attersoll Gifford, who is said to have written of him as a *"low-born churl who has dared to marry into my family"*. It must have been an awkward and unhappy period for both lovers who were still resolved to marry despite the opposition. The bitter experience was later expressed in his poem *I Rose And Went To Rou'tor Town*.

It is more likely, however, that Hardy went directly to stay with the Serjeants, good friends of Emma's, who lived at St Benet's Abbey, Lanivet. It was here, in the summer-house, that Hardy wrote several chapters of his first serialised book, *A Pair of Blue Eyes*.

Extract from
Emma Hardy's
Some Recollections
1911
▼

In Victorian times there was a lucrative market for new authors to publish their work in instalments in popular magazines. That year Hardy earned twice what he could have done through architecture in the same period and began to feel confident about making his living from literature.

At the close of 1872, Hardy was approached by the editor of the *Cornhill Magazine* who requested a serial for its readers. The first instalment of *Far From the Madding Crowd* was published anonymously, but by the end of the serial its success had promoted Hardy to the forefront of contemporary novelists.

Hardy and Emma met twice more in Cornwall during 1873. The Christmas of that year was the last time they stayed at St Juliot together.

"The day we were married was a perfect September day - 17th, 1874 - not a brilliant sunshine, but wearing a soft, sunny luminousness; just as it should be.

I have had various experiences, interesting some, sad others, since that lovely day, but all showing that an Unseen Power of great benevolence directs my ways..."

By the end of 1874, it was clear that *Far From the Madding Crowd* was a financial triumph. Now, with an income assured as long as he kept writing, Hardy and Emma decided to tie the knot.

They were married in September, not in their beloved Cornwall or in Emma's childhood town of Plymouth, but at St Peter's, Paddington. The service was conducted by Emma's uncle, the Canon of Worcester, and she was given away by her brother Walter. No other members of the Gifford or the Hardy families were present.

After a few days spent in Brighton they journeyed abroad for the very first time, to Paris and Rouen, for their honeymoon.

Throughout their long, ultimately ill-matched and fruitless marriage, they never returned to Cornwall.

Over the next ten years the Hardy's moved through a succession of rented rooms and houses in London and Dorset. Hardy wrote *The Return of the Native* and was increasingly invited to appear in fashionable and bohemian society. Emma did not always approve but Hardy, despite his lifelong shyness, continued to attend venues which would help further his reputation and his career.

In 1880, whilst writing *A Laodicean* for *Harper's Magazine*, Hardy became seriously ill, suffering an internal haemorrhage. After five months of being nursed by Emma, which did little to heal the growing rift between them, they moved again to Dorset, this time to Wimborne Minster. Here Hardy wrote some short stories and planned his next novel *Two on a Tower*.

After one last move to rented accommodation Hardy bought a plot of land on the outskirts of Dorchester. Here he designed and built Max Gate, an imposing red brick Victorian villa, where they finally settled.

He immersed himself again in the stories, traditions and history of the Dorset he had known as a boy. Much of this research found its way into his next novel, *The Mayor of Casterbridge*, completed in 1885 and published the following year. This was closely followed by *The Woodlanders*, which was well received by most critics and the reading public.

▲
Thomas Hardy
1880

Thomas Hardy, aged 55, 1895
▼

The success of *The Woodlanders* should have marked the beginning of a golden career for Hardy, but instead the next decade was the darkest of his entire life.

He continued writing short stories which he constantly had to edit, much to his frustration, to suit the taste or accepted 'morality' of Victorian readers. Although Hardy did not ever seek to scandalise, he wanted to portray life honestly and in its entirety, including the often complex nature of sexual relations.

In 1888 he began work on *Tess of the d'Urbervilles* and was determined to publish it in its original form. It was turned down by several magazine publishers on grounds of indecency. Hardy refused to omit the offending episodes, but eventually, in 1891, he gave in and re-wrote the novel in an acceptably sexless and watered-down form for the *Graphic* magazine. The story caused a sensation and the first book-edition (with much of the original material reinstated) quickly sold out.

Hardy was launched into the centre of a public furore and the unwelcomed attention and criticism hurt him deeply.

In 1893, he agreed to produce another serial which *"could not offend the most fastidious maiden"*. But when his completed work, *Jude the Obscure,* was released in book form two years later it too caused a scandal. Its unflattering references to Christian marriage attracted the most violent reactions. The Bishop of Wakefield wrote in the press, *"I bought one of Mr Hardy's novels, but was so disgusted with its insolence and indecency that I threw it into the fire"*, Hardy noted, *"probably in his despair at not being able to burn me."* Sensitive to these hostile reactions, and made financially secure by the success of both *Tess* and *Jude*, Hardy returned to his first love, poetry, producing in all eight volumes of poems.

The criticism of marriage expressed in *Jude* no doubt came from personal experience as Hardy's own relationship stagnated. Emma, who was sure the readers would see this aspect of the plot as being autobiographical, was mortified. She was also deeply offended by Hardy's attacks on religion and is even said to have strived to prevent *Jude*'s publication.

The difference of their characters created an unbearable tension between them, added to by their childlessness. Emma was vain, opinionated and a snob who felt that she had married beneath her social position.

Hardy on the other hand felt he had married an intellectual inferior, was embarrassed by her literary efforts and made no public recognition of her valuable contributions to his work. He was an intensely private man and was not ideally suited to the intimacy of marriage, feeling increasingly smothered by it. The reality of matrimony did not compare to the romantic, idealistic love he celebrated in his verses, many of which were included in the collection *Wessex Poems*, published in 1898.

▲ Emma Hardy aged 55, 1895

Within a year of this volume's release, the Boer War broke out, turning his thoughts to the history of conflict

Emma (seated), with Florence Dugdale standing next to her, in the summer of 1911
▼

and to man's struggle against fate. In 1904 he published the first part of his epic-drama of the Napoleonic Wars, *The Dynasts*, the final part of which appeared in 1908.

In 1910 he received the Order of Merit, one of many honours given to him.

Whilst working on *The Dynasts*, Hardy met Florence Emily Dugdale, who helped him with his research. She became indispensable to both him and Emma, doing secretarial work and then helping to run Max Gate.

In old age Hardy and Emma lived very separate lives, he often going to London for long periods and she retiring to an attic room in Max Gate where she slept.

In the Autumn of 1912, Emma was noted to be weaker and often complained of her heart though she was not noticeably ill. But on her birthday, the 24th of November, she became depressed and remarked that she felt unwell. On the 25th Emma took to her bed and the next day agreed to see the doctor. He did not think there was anything seriously wrong except that she was suffering from indigestion. The following day the maid found her moaning and very ill, requesting Hardy to come immediately to her side. He was working in his study and, after reprimanding the maid for a crooked collar, tidied his desk and followed her to Emma's room in the attic. When he saw his wife's face, he immediately hurried to her side asking *"Em, Em, don't you know me? It's Tom."*

No reply came from her lips and within five minutes her breathing softened and ceased. She had died from heart failure due to impacted gall stones.

Emma was buried at Stinsford Church near Dorchester, on the 30th of November, attended by a small congregation of mourners. Hardy's wreath was accompanied by an inscription *"From her lonely husband - with the old affection."*

After Emma's death, Hardy, filled with remorse and grief, was shocked by how much her loss affected him. He found among her possessions, her *Recollections* of their meeting and carefree courtship all those years ago.

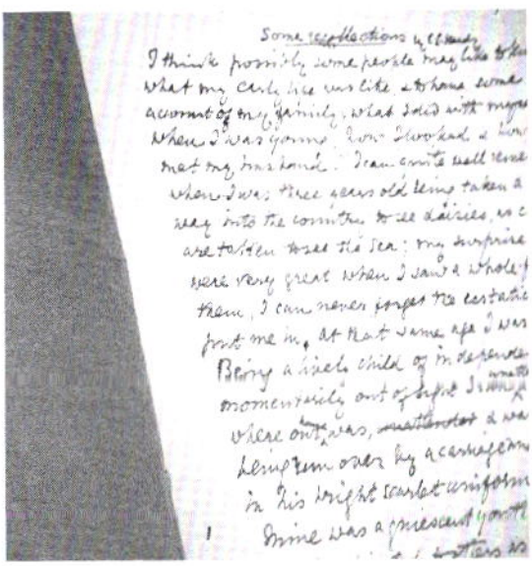

◄ Emma's notebook of recollections

In a desperate attempt to regain those feelings and to look beyond the failure of their later life, he travelled back to Cornwall, to revisit the places where they had been happy together. *"I have a faculty... for burying an emotion in my heart or brain for forty years, and exhuming it at the end of that time as fresh as when interred."* *(The Life of Thomas Hardy)*

Extract from Hardy's *The Life of Thomas Hardy* ▼

In March 1913, 43 years after his first trip almost to the day, Hardy returned to St Juliot. Then, as now, he must have found little altered. Beeny Cliff, the caves, the breakers, the salt air, the *"crooked ways"* and *"stiles of stone"* were still as he would have remembered.

The only element missing from the scene was the figure of Emma.

"There was one nook, indeed, which in some respects was pre-eminently the place where she might have lain - the graveyard of St Juliot, Cornwall - whose dilapidated old church had been the cause of their meeting, and in whose precincts the early scenes of their romance had a brief being."

In the poem *A Death-Day Recalled*, Hardy rebukes the familiar places that showed no response to the death *"of their former friend"*.

"Beeny did not quiver, / Juliot grew not gray, / Thin Vallency's river / Held its wonted way. / Bos seemed not to utter / Dimmest note of dirge, / Targan mouth a mutter / To its creamy surge."

One poem, composed in 1913, sums up Hardy's feelings about the wild, north Cornwall landscape and of falling in love with the woman who seemed so much a part of it.

"A ghost-girl-rider. And though, toil-tried, / He withers daily, / Time touches her not, / But she still rides gaily / In his rapt thought / On that shagged and shaly / Atlantic spot, / And as when first eyed / Draws rein and sings to the swing of the tide."
(The Phantom Horsewoman)

This journey resulted in an outpouring of twenty one of his most emotional poems published in one sequence called simply, *Poems of 1912-13*.

Thomas Hardy, aged 73, 1913 ▼

In all, Hardy wrote more than a hundred poems about Emma.

In 1914, at the age of 73, Hardy did what he termed *"the wisest thing to do"* and married Florence Dugdale who was almost 40 years his junior.

Her role at Max Gate seems to have continued in much the same vein as before, managing the household and filtering the constant demands on Hardy's time by uninvited guests.

Hardy's last visit to St Juliot and Cornwall, was in September, 1916. On the north wall of the church is the stone memorial to Emma, which he had ordered from a local stone mason. After inspecting it he wrote *The Marble Tablet*.

▲ Emma's memorial, designed by Hardy in 1913

"There it stands, though alas, what a little of her / Shows in its cold white look! / Not her glance, glide, or smile; not a tittle of her / Voice like the purl of a brook; / Not her thoughts, that you read like a book."

Following the trip he began *The Famous Tragedy of the Queen of Cornwall*, written solely for the Hardy Players - a group of amateur actors from Dorchester. *"My little play - 53 years in contemplation"* was his final homage to Emma in the guise of the Cornish Queen Iseult.

Thomas Hardy shortly before his death ▼

The last years of Hardy's life were spent mainly in seclusion, revising and arranging his earlier work into several collections. He also studiously destroyed personal papers and manuscripts which may have been of later use to biographers, including Emma's own recollections, diaries and an intriguing article entitled *What I*

Think of My Husband. At the same time, he compiled a carefully selected set of memoirs, the *The Early Life of Thomas Hardy 1840 - 1891* and *The Later Years of Thomas Hardy 1892 - 1928* (ostensibly written by Florence Hardy).

At the close of 1927, Hardy told Florence that he had done all he wanted to do. He took to his bed and grew progressively weaker until, on the evening of January 11th, he died.

His ashes were interred with due ceremony at Westminster Abbey, but his heart lies buried in Emma's grave in the quiet cemetery of Stinsford church.

The grave of Thomas, Emma and Florence Hardy in Stinsford churchyard, near Dorchester, Dorset ▼

A Pair of Blue Eyes

A *Pair of Blue Eyes* was mostly written during 1872-3 as a serial for *Tinsley's Magazine*, for which Hardy was paid £200. The serial appeared from September 1872 to July 1873 and was illustrated by J.A. Pasquier. The first episode was composed in London to meet the deadline for publication and the proofs were corrected whilst Hardy was visiting Cornwall in August, 1872. On his return to London, writing progress was slow, so Hardy retreated to the comparative peace of Dorset to finish the book.

As was the usual practice, the novel was published in a three-volume format in May, 1873, before the instalments were completed. It was the first work to bear Thomas Hardy's name and throughout his life-time it remained a personal favourite.

Like much of Hardy's other prose and poems, *A Pair of Blue Eyes* is set in his imaginary landscape of 'Wessex'. Over the following 50 years Hardy returned again and again to revise the text, subtly altering the details and making clearer the correspondences between his imaginary 'Off Wessex' and the real county of Cornwall.

Extract from Thomas Hardy's *A Pair of Blue Eyes*, 1873
▼

Anyone familiar with Cornish topography will recognise the disguised place-names within the pages: Castle Boterel is Boscastle; Dundagel is Tintagel; St Launce's is Launceston; Endelstow Rectory is St Juliot's Rectory etc. All of these are locations that would have become known to Hardy on his visits to the county whilst courting Emma Gifford. Many scenes in the novel can be traced to the landscape around Boscastle. Here, it is possible for the reader to see the same views and traverse the same ground as Elfride Swancourt or Henry Knight, lending a tangibility to their fictional world.

"These eyes were blue; blue as autumn distance - blue as the blue we see between the retreating mouldings of hills and woody slopes on a sunny September morning. A misty and shady blue, that had no beginning or surface, and was looked into rather than at."

The 'eyes' in the title of the book belong to Elfride Swancourt (daughter of the Rector of West Endelstow), the vivacious but naive heroine of the plot and pivotal figure in its complex love-triangle. The two men who pursue her are Stephen Smith, a young, attractive architect and Henry Knight, an older, learned essayist. Elfride, whose personality is described as... *"no more pervasive than that of a kitten"* is torn between the expectations of her suitors and Victorian society, and the desires of her own heart which she does not always seem to understand.

Smith, although hard working and ambitious, is held back by his lowly origins. Elfride's father opposes the love-match so the young couple elope. However, due to Elfride's indecision, they do not go through with the marriage; indeed Elfride never gets beyond the station in London, heading straight back to Plymouth within ten minutes of her arrival. Striving to better his social position and become a man worthy of the hand of Elfride, Stephen accepts a post in India confident that his sweetheart will remain faithful... *"For ever - to the end of her life!"*

Knight, on the other hand, is the epitome of Victorian respectability and gradually wins Elfride's affection in Stephen's absence. He knows nothing of her previous attachment and sees her as the embodiment of womanly virtue and purity, satisfying his taste for... *"untried lips."* After the dramatic scene on the *"Cliff without a Name"*, when Elfride saves Knight's life, the two become engaged. When he eventually learns of her past tryst, he (mistakenly) assumes that she and Stephen had been lovers and breaks off their marriage plans.

Through her fickleness the heart-broken Elfride loses both her admirers and her chance of future happiness and is left on a course destined to end in tragedy, dying within a few months of her marriage to Lord Luxellian.

Through the relationships of the central characters Hardy explores conflicts of morality and social consciousness, desire and sexual restraint, the accepted roles of men and women and the strict class distinctions which pervaded Victorian society.

This novel, above all others, is of interest because of the strong parallels evident between the circumstances of the plot and Hardy's own life.

Aspects of Hardy's character can be discerned in both the leading men. Firstly, in Stephen Smith, the ardent and self-improving young architect; and then in Henry Knight, the erudite but emotionally repressed man of letters, who like Hardy was a late developer... *"in virility, while mentally precocious"*; whilst in Elfride Swancourt we can see the young Emma Gifford, with her charm and vivacity, her naivety and joy of riding her pony recklessly over the Cornish landscape. Other autobiographical elements include the boat journey to Plymouth, taken from Hardy's own recent voyage; and Mr Swancourt's disapproval of the match between Elfride and Smith (echoing Mr Gifford's objections to Hardy's marriage proposal to Emma). Even the tense climax on the cliff may have been suggested by a personal experience recollected from Emma's childhood.

▶
Illustration for *A Pair of Blue Eyes* by W.J. Morgan in 1882-3.

"I often dream of the dangerous pathways over cliffs and rocks leading to spots almost inaccessible. Once I hung over the 'devil's hole' by a tuft of grass whilst my schoolfellow shouted to a mussel-seeking man far below, who rushed up the steep ascent and rescued me..."

▲
Extract from Emma's *Some Recollections*, 1911

It is clear from the detailed descriptions that the looming, primeval landscape of this part of the county made a deep impression on Hardy. The romance of place inspired him to use it as his *"theatre for these imperfect dramas of country life and passions."*

Hardy sums up his feelings for the area in his 1895 preface to the novel...

" The place is pre-eminently (for one person at least) the region of dream and mystery. The ghostly birds, the pall-like sea, the frothy wind, the eternal soliloquy of the waters, the bloom of dark purple cast that seems to exhale from the shoreward precipices, in themselves lend to the scene an atmosphere like the twilight of a night vision."

The Walk

"Why go to Saint - Juliot? What's Juliot to me?
Some strange necromancy
But charmed me to fancy
That much of my life claims the spot as its key.

Does there even a place like Saint - Juliot exist?
Or a Vallency Valley
With stream and leafed alley,
Or Beeny, or Bos with its flounce flinging mist?"

(First and last stanza of *A Dream or No*)

Walking the same paths today, treading in the Hardys' footsteps, the magic of these places can still be felt. The church, the valley, the stream and the wild cliffs are all there as he described them, and have lost none of their power to enchant and fire the imagination.

Distance: Approx. 8 miles

Average Time: 5 hours

Degree of Difficulty: Strenuous in parts

Boscastle village 1870
▼

In 1870 when he first came here, Boscastle's population of 360 individuals was largely self sufficient, the economy dependent mainly on the bustling harbour and surrounding farms. There was a thriving community of traders including ship owners, merchants, fishermen, sailors, carriers, grocers, inn keepers, ironmongers, butchers, bakers, tailors, drapers, shoe makers, maltsters, millers, carpenters, blacksmiths, masons, farmers, clergy, surgeons, solicitors, a chemist and druggist, school master, harbour master, post master, accountant, even a land surveyor. Although this life has long since disappeared, Boscastle still retains much of its old character and charm.

Hopefully, this route will give you an insight into how Boscastle and its countryside appeared to Hardy when he visited a century and more ago.

Maps showing the route and the extracted directions start on page 75.

Starting from the car park, head down towards the harbour, passing the Cobweb Inn on your right.

This building dates back to the 1700s and in 1790 was licenced to store and sell beer, wine and spirits. Known as the Launceston Cellar, it was run by the wine merchants Messrs. Sloggatt & Rosevear and was at one time one of eighteen ale houses in the village. In around 1801, a fully laden vessel owned by these wealthy merchants evaded a French privateer and came safely into the harbour. In gratitude for this narrow escape, the merchants built a teetotal Methodist Chapel on Fore Street, which is still active today.

▲ Boscastle village 1870

The Cobweb circa 1947 ▼

In Hardy's time, flour and corn was stored in the upper lofts of the Cobweb building, whilst alcohol was bottled and casked on its lower floor. It was not until 1947 that it was finally licensed and turned into an inn. Several centuries of accumulated cobwebs that hung from the ceiling were saved in the conversion, hence the unusual name.

The Wellington Hotel in the 1860s
▼

Continue down towards the harbour.

The pottery next door to the Cobweb was once the bakery. Next to that, is the Old Manor House, which was the home and office of the Boscastle Estate Manager, where property business was undertaken and tenants paid their rents. Bridge Walk shops on your left are a relatively new development and replaced a tall building known as Wards & Sons Stores. Opposite, running at an angle to the road, is the cobbled lane of Valency Row. In the 19th century this was the main route to the harbour and many of the houses that fronted onto the busy street were inns and malt-houses, including The Ship Inn, now a private residence.

This inn is well documented by the Rev. R. S. Hawker, who stayed there in his youth. The landlady at that time was a ruddy-faced widow by the name of Joan Treworgy. Its parlour, where customers dined, was described as *"rather cosy than magnificent"* and the guest bedroom was reached by a cabin-ladder. Here Hawker and a friend spent an uncomfortable night, the room being *"small hot, stuffy"* and *"the whole atmosphere of the village was impregnated with onions and cheese."* Their bill came to: *"T for 2.. 6s., Sleep for 2.. 1s., Meat and taties and bier.. 1s.6d and Bresks.. 1s.6d".*

In Hardy's day, The Ship was run by William Bluett, it was one of five inns found in Boscastle, at the time, the other four being, The Brigg, The Boscastle, The Napoleon and The Wellington Hotel.

The Wellington Hotel circa 1912

When you reach the road bridge, notice The Wellington Hotel on your left.

Originally known as the Bos Castle Hotel, it is one of the oldest coaching inns in north Cornwall with parts dating back to the 1600s. Renamed in 1852 as the Scott's Wellington Hotel, it was largely rebuilt the following year and further extended in 1860 by its owner William Scott, to accommodate the increasing tourist trade. In a guidebook dating back to 1916, Boscastle is mentioned as having... *"one good hotel (Wellington) where coach passengers can break their journey; there are also some small boarding-houses, and many that let lodgings where goodwill goes far to make up for rough accommodation".*

Guests arrived here by horse drawn coaches as late as 1926, making it one of the last staging posts in Britain. Thomas Hardy is reputed to be one of a number of prominent persons to have stayed here. Edward VII with a 'lady friend', is believed to have been in a royal party at the hotel in the 1870s and Sir Henry Irving, the great English actor of his time, often stayed here. It is said that he visited a certain Boscastle woman endowed with magical powers (some say she was a witch) who advised him on his career moves. He even gave her an allowance, paid quarterly by the local doctor's wife. Unfortunately, her gifts failed to further the actor's fortunes and Irving died penniless in 1905.

Sir Henry Irving

Quaytown circa 1880 ▼

Displayed within the hotel are a set of stained glass windows commissioned to commemorate Queen Victoria's visit to the then County Town of Bodmin in 1846. Also, some of the original brass and ruby glass oil lamps installed by Hardy in his renovation of St Juliot church in 1872 can be seen.

The overshot watermill adjacent to the Wellington, dates back from the early 19th century and is mentioned in Hardy's diary dated Thursday, March 10th, 1870. Its two wheels were driven by a leat from the Valency River and were used for grinding corn until 1946, when the mill was sold.

An old attractive cottage once stood on the corner of the bridge opposite, before the road was widened and the bridge rebuilt following a devastating flood in 1957.

Cross over the road and follow the lane that runs along the north bank of the river.

The array of buildings on both sides of the river were originally warehouses and workshops *"all the appliances of a busy trading port"*. The assorted shops on your right were coal stores until 1922, the gift shops further on were ship's chandlers. The Old Forge at the far end of Valency Row was the village smithy where wheelwrights from the carpenters shop on the other side of the river brought their wagon wheels to be iron bound. Next to it stands the limekiln, where limestone or chalk was burnt to make quicklime.

This was used in mortar for building purposes and more extensively as an agricultural top dressing, to sweeten the acid soils of the farmsteads in the area.

The building that today houses the National Trust Boscastle Visitor Centre, has had many previous uses, including a rope locker, village hall, carpenter's shop and restaurant. However its original 19th century function was as a fish cellar, where pilchards were salted, pressed and packed for export to Mediterranean countries. The adjoining National Trust shop and cafe was also a cellar, whilst the Witchcraft Museum was a mineral store and shipping warehouse.

When Hardy first came to the village, the harbour was experiencing its heyday, with as many as 300 ships of up to 100 tons visiting here per annum. Up to thirteen vessels docked here at any one time; these included schooners, sloops, smacks and ketches.

The harbour's narrow entrance was notoriously difficult to manoeuvre under sail. To make the task easier a 30ft 'hobbling boat', crewed by seven men, would row out to incoming ships with a 'warping rope' which a shore party would then haul on to guide them into safety.

▲ Hobbling boat guiding a trading vessel into the harbour circa 1900

Trade stretched over the waters to America, Ireland, France, Belgium, London, Liverpool, South Wales etc and passenger ships belonging to Jabez Brown and Co. regularly sailed to and from Bristol.

In 1870, 4000 tons of coal was imported, along with 250 tons of wine, beer and spirits, 150 tons of brick, 150 tons of groceries, 200 tons of timber, 130 tons of iron, 80 tons of tiles, 300 tons of manure and 150 tons of

Boscastle Harbour with Profile Rock circa 1870
▼

corn. As for exports, 50 tons of corn, 50 tons of slate and 250 tons of China clay were shipped out from here. Even today, wheel marks of the myriad of horse drawn carts and wagons that carried these goods to and fro, can still be seen in the river bed. The whole place buzzed with activity.

As you approach the lower bridge, bear right and head up towards Penally Terrace.

This newly erected bridge, constructed as part of the Boscsatles Flood Prevention Scheme, replaced a structure that was built in 1887. This in turn had replaced a crude wooden walkway that served the community of craftsmen on both banks.

The Harbour Lights on your left, was one of four buildings to be washed away in the 2004 floods. The original structure dated back to the 16th century and was reputedly a pig sty in Hardy's time. Pigs were an important part of the local economy in those days and annexed to almost every human abode was a small pigsty. Boscastle even had its own 'pig spooker' whose trade was to ring their noses. The bartering of half a pig for enough salt to cure the other half was a common practice, the sea salt being collected from what is known locally as the 'bathing pool', which can still be seen on the seaward side of the harbour wall.

Beyond stands the present-day YHA which was known in Hardy's time as the Palace Stables. The harbour's many working horses were housed here.

Continue up the rise.

Profile Rock, which can be seen at the end of the headland, was described by Hardy as "*vulturine*". Some say it resembles Queen Victoria, others, that it is the profile of Napoleon. Whichever, it is a prominent feature and one which gives an indication of the complexity of the geology here.

An hour on either side of low tide, it is worth looking out for the blow hole which issues from below the point. The sea, having formed a tunnel through the neck of the headland, forces itself through exploding with a rush of air and spray. Hardy in his poem *The Re-Enactment* writes of it...

"*When the boom / Of the ocean, like a hammering in a hollow tomb, / Throbbed up the copse-clothed valley / From the shore*"
and in the poem *The Wind's Prophecy*, it is likened to a giant snoring.

Penally Terrace was built for sea captains. The courtyard behind was once a fish cellar with sail lofts above.

Penally Terrace, seen from the south side of the river circa 1900 ▼

In the 19th century Cornwall was the world's capital of the herring and pilchard fishing industry. Like most of the fishing villages that dot this coastline, men and women worked in fish cellars like these from dawn to dusk, 'bulking' fish. Shoals of pilchards would arrive off the coast around April and as the season advanced their numbers increased until, by mid summer, they were present in

The harbour with its original outer wall circa 1880 ▼

vast abundance, affirmed by the saying... *"When the corn is in the shock / Then the fish are off the rock"*. It was said that the whole sea would change colour with their numbers and that in one day alone a staggering 75 million were once caught off St Ives. Although a good many were eaten fresh, the bulk was cured and exported to Italy, Spain and the plantation colonies of the West Indies. Barrels were partly filled with alternate layers of salt and fish, then pressed by large stones hung from beams slotted into niches in the walls. The fish were left for a month, then washed & re-packed into hogsheads. The oil that drained off was sold separately and was used to light the streets of Britain's cities.

From Penally Terrace, follow the path leading up the north side of the harbour.

Alongside the path are numerous seats hewn from the rock. These date from circa 1849, when a certain Mr Fuggard, at his own expense, commissioned paths, excavations and seating to be placed for the benefit of those *"persons desirous of improving their health with a few months residence on the northern coast, and by others who have taste for the beautiful and romantic character of the scenery which it presents"*.

Ascend to the flagpole on the top of Penally Hill (288 ft).

Looking south, gives an excellent view of the harbour. In spite of its exposed condition and difficult access for large sailing vessels, the harbour was of considerable importance in olden days.

The inner pier is known to have been destroyed twice before 1584 when Sir Richard Grenville of the 'Revenge' fame, rebuilt it at a cost of £200. It was restored in 1740 and has since remained virtually unaltered. The outer bar was built in 1820 to help kerb the violent sea swells. This breakwater was damaged by a mine during the Second World War and the present structure dates from 1962.

From Penally Hill there are also magnificent views along the coast towards Tintagel with sweeping fields rolling inland. The cliffs on the southern side of the harbour, stretching as far as Trebarwith Strand, were in Hardy's time, extensively quarried for slate. At quarries such as Grower Quarry, Boscastle Quarry, California Quarry and Welltown Quarry, men were lowered down by a system of ropes and cables to foothold ledges where they then worked the surface with hammers and chisels. The cut stone was then winched down chains anchored to the sea bed and lowered into the holds of awaiting boats.

The building that stands squarely on the skyline, is the Camelot Castle Hotel which was built in 1898 as a response to the influx of visitors to Tintagel. Like other authors, poets and artists Hardy was fascinated by Tintagel's connection with the Arthurian legend. The island, according to local tradition and as Hardy believed, is the final resting place of Queen Iseult (from the Celtic legend of Tristram and Iseult) and is the setting for Hardy's poetic drama *The Famous Tragedy of the Queen of Cornwall.*

Looking inland, the church tower a mile or so away is that of Trevalga. This small hamlet

Hardy's poetic drama *The Famous Tragedy of the Queen of Cornwall* (1923) ▼

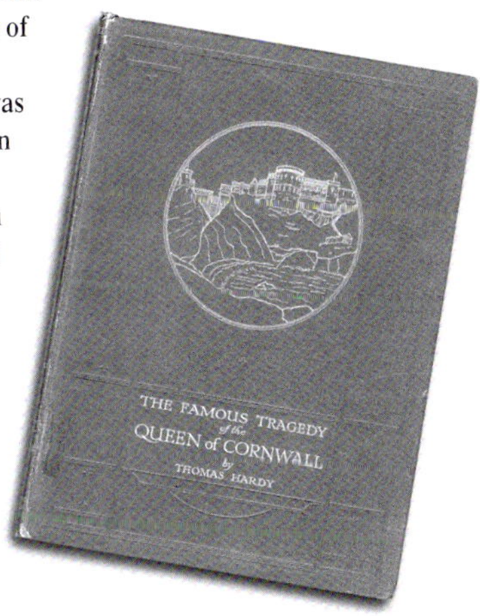

dates back to the Domesday Book and has remarkably preserved an air of timelessness. Dedicated to St Petroc, its Norman church has withstood Atlantic gales since the 13th century.

On the far side of the harbour entrance is a white, turreted building on top of Willapark headland.

This was built as a 'pleasure house' circa 1827 by Thomas Avery, a wealthy local merchant, who in 1840 purchased the entire Manor Estate of Boscastle. The building was later used as a coastguard lookout post. The bold promontory that it stands on still bears evidence of an Iron Age defensive settlement.

Further examples of ancient history in the area can be seen inland on Forrabury Common, with its well preserved Celtic field system known as The Stitches. Forty-two strips in all, each plot is cultivated with individual crops such as corn, potatoes or hay from Lady Day (25 March) to Michaelmas (29 September), then the land is left to rest during the winter months with livestock allowed to roam and graze freely.

Beyond the Common, the tower of Forrabury Church can just be seen. Immortalised in Rev. R.S. Hawker's poem *The Silent Tower Of Bottreaux*, the verses retell the tale of a ship bearing bells for the church. Nearing the end of its journey and about to enter the safe haven of Boscastle, the pilot thanked God for a safe passage. The blasphemous captain, on hearing this, mocked him, saying that it was he and a good ship that should

The bell-less tower of Forrabury Church circa 1900 ▼

be thanked, whereupon a great storm arose. The ship, the bells and all on board perished beneath the waves, all but the pious pilot. Dedicated to St Symphorian, the church dates back to Norman times, but of this original structure only the tower, porch and south side remains, as it was extended and rebuilt in 1867.

The isolated rock just outside the harbour is named The Meachard and it was here that ships too large to enter the port were anchored - the mooring rings still survive.

The geology here is extremely complex. It is a mixture of slates, sandstones, shales and volcanic intrusions. On top of this considerable folding and buckling, brought about by the movement of the earth's plates, has produced stunning patterns in the rock face.

The flagpole, said to be an old mast rescued from a local shipwreck, can be seen for miles around and the fish shaped weather vane reveals the wind direction for boatmen in the harbour below.

From Penally Hill walk along the coastal footpath heading north towards Pentargon following hedges of weathered stones. It is worth looking to your right for the panoramic views over the whole village, particularly up the Jordan Valley.

The grassy site of Bottreaux Castle can be seen above the Wellington Hotel. The flat platform where the Norman Baron, William de Bottreaux built his castle between 1080 and 1117 is all that remains today, but in 1873, Sir John Maclean described the location thus... *"On the lower, or northern side, the sites of the outer and of the inner walls are very distinguishable."*

Boscastle village and the Jordan Valley, 1904. ▼

Stormy waters off north Cornwall
▼

Continue along the coastal footpath. Ahead lies Pentargon, Beeny and Fire Beacon Point, on top of which you will eventually climb. Beyond lies Cambeak, Hartland Point and on a clear day, 33 miles away, Lundy Island can be seen.

It is hard to believe on calm days that this shoreline has been the grave of countless ships and sailors. The Rev. R.S. Hawker of Morwenstow wrote... *"From Padstow Point to Lundy Light / Is a watery grave by day or night"*, and between 1823 and 1846 alone, some 130 ships were lost here.

The author, Sabine Baring Gould described these waters as *"... emphatically 'the cruel sea,' fierce, insatiate, hungering for human lives and stately vessels, that it may cast them up mumbled and mangled after having robbed them of life and treasure."* He goes on... *"It is a rainy coast. It is said in Devon, and the same is true here, The West wind comes and brings us rain, / The East wind blows it back again; / The South wind brings us rainy weather, / The North wind cold and rain together."*

A small newspaper cutting found in an old guidebook to Boscastle dated 1866, with a scribbled date of Dec. '74 beside it, is headlined *"Loss of a steamer with all hands."* It reads... *"Boscastle, the mountainous cliffs of which are a barrier to the sea on the wildest part of the north coast of Cornwall, has just witnessed the doom of another gallant ship."* The steamer whose lights were seen approaching the harbour, is believed to have been the 'SS Alliance' of Cardiff and of the 25 men on board, none survived to tell the tale of the

ship's destruction. Since safe havens are scarce along these northern shores, Boscastle has played an important role as a port of refuge for many centuries.

Notice the old stone hedge that accompanies you along this trail, with its massive quartz foundations and tightly packed, vertical slate stones emulating the geology of the surrounding cliff face.

Pentargon is a most dramatic place and is featured in Hardy's poem *After a Journey*. In 1913, he made a pilgrimage here and the poem describes a night vigil spent in the cove where he is haunted by Emma's ghostly presence. Dark brooding cliffs surround an echoing pebble beach and the dramatic waterfall free-falls from the top of the cliff down 120ft to the rocks below.

▲ A dramatic 19th century etching of Pentargon waterfall

Hardy describes it in the novel *A Pair of Blue Eyes* as... *"The small stream here found its death. Running over the precipice it was dispersed in spray before it was half way down, and falling like rain upon projecting ledges, made minute grassy meadows of them. Lower down it soaked away amid the débris of the cliff. This was the inglorious end of the river."* In Hardy's time it was possible to descend to the beach at Pentargon and according to local sayings the bathing was good, but a series of landslides from the 1930s onwards has made that impossible and today the only approach is by boat. One of the features of Pentargon that Hardy possibly visited is a large cave, which tunnels 200ft into the cliff on the north side of the bay and is known as Double Doors.

This was once a great tourist attraction and W. Wood in his book *The Strangers Handbook to Cornwall*, dated 1866, notes... *"The most striking object of this place is an extensive cavern, about a mile east of the harbour."*

(**Short-cut:** Above Pentargon, one can return to Boscastle by taking a path across the fields towards the Bude road. To avoid the traffic, use the footpath that runs parallel to the road and then continue along the Green Cut path, back into the village - a round trip of about two and a half miles).

To continue on the long route: leave Pentargon behind, climb the footpath to the top of the headland and then descend the steep-sided valley out to Beeny Cliff.

Once well grazed, this cliff land is beginning to lose some of its wildlife interest as the coarser grass and vegetation takes over. However, there is still much to enjoy along this stretch, not least the wildflowers that survive. Below, fulmars or peregrines might glide past whilst on the other side of Pentargon, you might glimpse guillemot and razorbill alighting on their rocky nests.

Hardy's sketch of Beeny Cliff with Emma in the foreground, 22nd of August 1870 ▼

The lairs of puffins, which Hardy mentions in his poem *The Interloper*, are now scarce on this coast and the choughs that Emma Hardy writes of in her *Recollections*, are sadly extinct in this part of Cornwall. In early autumn, huge flocks of goldfinches can be seen here as they feed on the seeds of gorse, heather and other wildflowers.

On the shoreline below these sheer cliffs are the aptly named, the Seal Caves, still the haunt of Atlantic grey seals. It was here, Emma recalled, that she and Thomas used to gaze *"down at the solemn small shores below where seals lived, coming out of great caverns very occasionally."*

Today, although not as common as in former times, seals' mournful songs can sometimes be heard and they may be seen basking on the rocks nearby.

Seals were once caught here and were served as food in some of the *"rough accommodation"* found in Boscastle, as recounted by the Rev. R.S. Hawker in 1867. He and a friend ate a meal, but were perplexed by the identity of the roasted meat served to them as *"Meat-nice wholesome meat and taties"*. At a later date Hawker discovered by way of an article in an *"... ancient history of Cornwall. Therein I read 'that the sillie people of Bouscastle and Boussiney do catch in the summer seas divers young soleys (seals), which, doubtful if they be fish or flesh, conynge housewives will nevertheless roast, and do make thereof very savoury meat.'"*

W. Wood in his book *The Strangers Handbook to Cornwall*, notes that *"... the sailors accustomed to the spot, generally take bars of iron and strike [the seals] over the nose, by which they are disabled, easily killed, and taken to Boscastle for their skins and oil."*

This is the landscape that made an indelible impression on Hardy and to which he returned four months after Emma's death. This is where she recollected carefree days... *" An unforgettable experience to me, scampering up and down the hills on my beloved mare alone, wanting no protection, the rain going down my back often and my hair floating on the wind."* This image of her is captured in Hardy's poem *Beeny Cliff* and the area appears in several of his *Poems of 1912-13*, it is also the setting for many of the scenes in *A Pair of Blue Eyes*.

▲ The Rev. R.S. Hawker

Here, his diary recalls the morning of Thursday, March 10th 1870 *"Went with E.L.G. to Beeny Cliff. She on horseback - .... On the cliff.... 'The tender grace of a day', etc. The run down to the edge. The coming home...."* This landscape and that morning are revisited some 43 years later and expounded in his poem *Beeny Cliff*. Three other poems *The Figure In The Scene*, *Why Did I Sketch* and *It Never Looks Like Summer* recall their second visit here on a wet Monday in August 1870.

From Beeny, climb the path to Fire Beacon Point.

Possibly the site of a signal beacon in the Elizabethan period, when lookouts were located all along the coast of Britain, ready to warn of an approaching Armada. It is quite a climb but well worth it for the magnificent views.

To the south, Tintagel Island can be seen, then following the coast, Tintagel's Willapark, the islands known as The Sisters, Fire Beacon Hill with Trevalga inland, Long and Short Island, then Boscastle's Willapark with its white turret and Penally Hill with the flagpole. To the north, High Cliff dominates the coastal scenery, standing at 731ft, it is the highest point on the coast in England. At the base of the grey cliffs are beaches known as The Strangles and Little Strand. Further on is the arched feature of Northern Door and the headland of Cambeak, behind which lies Crackington Haven and the shores of Bude Bay, stretching past Millook, Widemouth, Bude, Cleave Camp Satellite Station, Morwenstow and finally Hartland.

Strike inland along the path at the end of the third field from Fire Beacon Point. (Should you wish to stand at the exact spot where Hardy, on Monday 22nd August 1870, sketched his Beeny Cliff in the driving rain, then follow the coastpath onwards for some 250 yards.)

To retrace the steps of the two lovers returning to St Juliot on that *"...slow wet walk, / By crooked ways, and over stiles of stone"* follow the hedge. It will lead you out past North

The Old Rectory of St Juliot ▼

Lodge onto a metalled road. Here turn right and follow the lane around a bend, downwards into the valley, passing the 18th century farmstead of Middle Beeny and the 16th century farmhouse of Lower Beeny on your right. Once you reach the valley, ignore the first marked footpath on your left. Cross over a culvert and a few yards ahead, follow the track up to a gate, to the left of which is a wooden stile. Keep ahead, across a field and along the farm track of Trebyla then out onto the main Boscastle to Bude road. Carefully cross the road and climb the stile directly in front, then veer 11 o'clock and follow the path across the field and on towards St Juliot. This path crosses five fields in all, over some ancient stiles and eventually emerges through a gate opposite Penventon Farm. To your left you can find the old Parish School, now converted into a private residence.

It was here that the parishioners of St Juliot worshipped during the work on the church and where, on the 11th of April 1872, lunch and teas were held in celebration of the opening of the newly restored building. The school master at the time was Abel French and the schoolmistress, whose duties were to teach the girls of the parish *"knitting and serving"*, was his Canadian wife Adalaide, a cripple from birth.

(Should you wish to see the Old Rectory of St Juliot, to which Thomas Hardy came in March 1870, then turn immediately right and drop down the drive.)

Recognisable as the rectory of West Endelstow in *A Pair of Blue Eyes*, Hardy describes this approach in Chapter Two as... *"a little dell lay like a nest at their feet, towards which the driver pulled the horse at a sharp*

St Juliot Church circa 1895 ▼

angle, and descended a steep slope which dived under the trees like a rabbit's burrow. They sank lower and lower."

The Old Rectory dates from 1847 and has remained virtually unchanged since Hardy first set eyes on the place on that fateful Monday, the 7th of March 1870. The times spent within these walls are remembered in numerous poems, such as *The Old Gown*, *The Curtains Now Are Drawn*, *At the Piano*, *Where They Lived*, *The Frozen Greenhouse*, *The Sundial On A Wet Day*, *Best Times* and *The Re-enactment* where Hardy pictures himself as a ghost returning in search of the past.

Today the Old Rectory is an award winning B & B and should you wish to stay, you would discover the charming interior with its pervasive air of history hardly changed from those courtship days. Hardy's own guest room, Emma's bedroom overlooking the garden, the parlour where they sang and played chess, the conservatory, all are in a remarkable state of preservation.

Resuming the walk to St Juliot Church from the gate opposite Penventon Farm, join the road and bear right, following it for some half a mile.

Snugly tucked away below the road, the isolated Church of St Juliot overlooks the upper reaches of the Valency Valley and its scattered farms. Some suggest that because of its shape and position on a spur, the churchyard was sited within an ancient 'round' - an Iron Age fort or settlement. It has certainly been a place of worship for over a millennium and was mentioned

in the Domesday Book (1086) as a secular manor, by the name Sanguiland, which implies an ecclesiastical site.

In 1238, the Chapel dedicated to St Julitta was acquired by the Canons of Launceston Priory.

The antiquity of the place is apparent with the ancient stone cross that greets you on the right of the gate. Known as Anderton Mill Cross, it is one of three in the churchyard. This wheel-headed cross was bought for the sum of two shillings and moved here in 1852 from the south side of the valley where it was in use as a gatepost (the leaded holes can still be seen on the shaft). Further down the path on your left is another wheel-headed cross known as Tregatheral Cross. Found in 1952 with its head buried in the ground, it again had been used as a gatepost at an old mill near Minster. It was removed here for preservation in 1953. The third cross is on its original site by the southern entrance to the churchyard. It is one of the best preserved wheel-headed crosses in Cornwall and is known as St Juliot's Cross.

When Hardy first walked into this churchyard on Tuesday the 8th of March 1870 it was at the time of year, some might say, when it is at its very best, with masses of snowdrops and daffodils drifting over the banks. The Tuesday was an austere grey day and a funeral was taking place; nevertheless Hardy stayed all day drawing and measuring the ruinous building. What Hardy found was a church in a perilous state, echoed by many of the churches in the area at the time.

Lake, in his *Parochial History of the County of Cornwall*, (published between 1868 and 1872) had this to say...
"Excepting the south aisle, extreme age has reduced this once superior church to a state of irremediable dilapidation; it is now 1868, closed for reconstruction.

"Thurston holds St Juliot from the Count. Edwy held it before 1066, and paid tax for 1 furlong (10 acres); 1 virgate (30 acres) of land there, however. Land for 3 ploughs; half plough there; 2 slaves. 2 villagers. Pastures, 30 acres. Formerly 7 shillings; value now 5 shillings. (2 cows)."

▲
1086 Domesday Book entry for St Juliot

The tower is of three stages; either through extreme age or as some say from being struck by lightning, it is in a ruinous and falling state. It contained five good bells, but these have latterly been removed to the north transept for preservation." Hardy wrote of these bells in his diary, on that first day... *"Man tolled the bell (which stood inverted on the ground in the neglected transept) by lifting the clapper and letting it fall against the side."* Emma reiterates the condition of the church in her *Recollections*... The church had suffered neglect and decay for many years. It was a poor parish as Emma noted *"where the belief in witchcraft was carried out in actual practice amongst the primitive inhabitants... Traditions and strange gossipings the common talk... and where hard labour upon the stony soil made a cold mostly ill-natured working class, yet with some good traits and fine exceptions."*

Drastic measures were needed to be taken and a decision as far back as 1854 stated *"with the exception of the walls of the South Aisle and Porch, an entire rebuilding will be necessary"*.

▲ The interior of St Juliot Church prior to restoration, with its carved bench ends

With this in mind Hardy set to work and the demolition of the tower, nave and chancel took place shortly after his second visit in August 1870. Hardy regretted in later years his involvement in destroying so much of the structure.

But in fairness his work is more harmonious and sympathetic to the past than the efforts of other contemporary architects, re-using where possible original stonework and wood and matching new windows with the old. He made careful instructions for repairing the entire chancel screen, marking on his drawings where scarfs and patches were to be applied. However, the enthusiasm and generosity of the builder overtook his wishes. Visiting the site one day, Hardy found a new, highly varnished screen in place. The builder explained *"I said to myself, I won't stand on a pound or two while I'm about it, and I'll give 'em a new screen instead of that patched-up old thing."* Other calamities occurred; a Saxon north door, which Hardy had made a drawing of, was accidentally destroyed and thirty six old bench ends disappeared. A similar fate occurred at nearby Minster Church which underwent extensive restoration at the same time. Bench ends and timber were sold for less than £1 a ton, and it is said that the actor, Sir Henry Irving, had a chair built for his London productions from Minster woodwork.

"The tower went on cracking from year to year and the bells remained in the little North Transept, their mouths open upward. The carved bench-ends rotted more and more, the ivy hung gaily from the roof-timbers and the birds and bats had a good time up there unmolested; no one seemed to care."

▲ Extract from Emma Hardy's *Some Recollections*

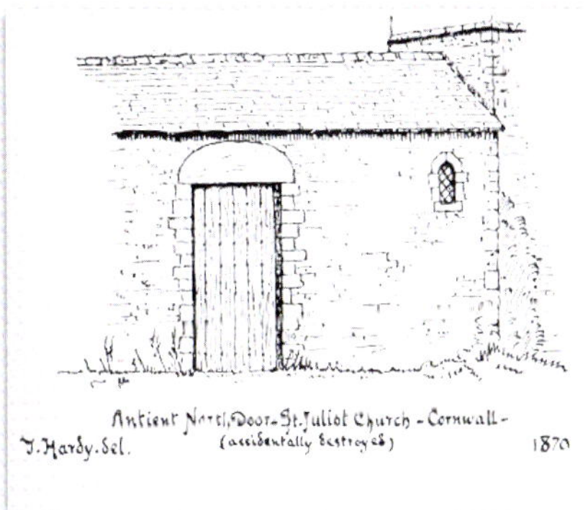

▲ Hardy's sketch of the Saxon north door, which was accidentally destroyed

After Emma, accompanied by local school children, laid the foundation stone, the rebuilding of St Juliot church began in earnest. By the spring of 1872 the work was complete and it was re-opened on the 11th of April in the presence of a large congregation and numerous clergy. It had a new three-staged tower on the site of the old, the nave and chancel had been replaced by a smaller north aisle and the 15th century former south aisle was now the chancel. The south porch with its fine Norman castellated roof remained untouched. The total expenditure was £1277.1s.5d.

St Juliot has changed very little since that day, except for the accumulated gravestones surrounding it.

Within the church are three wall tablets of interest. The commemorative tablet to Emma Hardy on the north wall, was designed by her husband and a local stonemason was commissioned to carve it in March 1913. In 1916, Hardy returned for his final visit to inspect it and consequently wrote two poems regarding the experience, *The Monument-Maker* and *The Marble Tablet*.

Memorial tablet at St Juliot's to Emma Hardy ▼

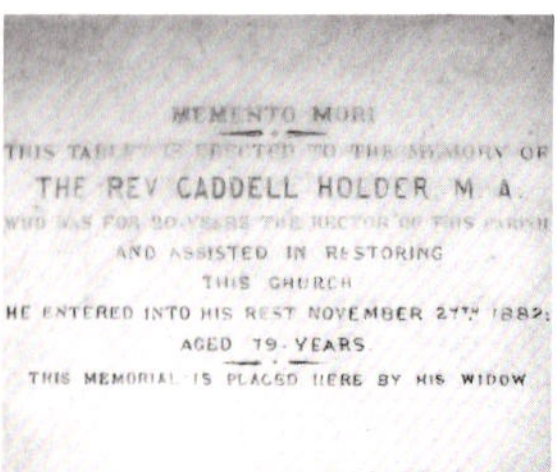

▲ Memorial tablet to the Rev. Caddell Holder

Next to Emma's memorial is a matching tablet, erected in 1928, also designed by Hardy, it records his association with the church and neighbourhood. The third tablet of interest is the memorial to Emma's brother-in-law, the Rector of St Juliot, the Rev. Caddell Holder (1803-1882). Emma wrote of him in her *Recollections*... *"My only sister married the Rev: Caddell Holder, son of a Judge of Barbadoes, where he was born: he often spoke of his beautiful home there with oranges growing by his bed-room window. At Trinity College Oxford he was a gentleman-commoner (this is now abolished), where his only privilege was being allowed to walk upon the grass and wear a gold-tasselled cap."* He was, according to Emma... *"somewhat delicate because of his West Indian birth. He was, however, very energetic, and a very Boagernes [Boanerges] in his preaching, which style was greatly relished by the simple folk of his scattered parish. In those days clergymen were very lax in their duties - but he was quite exact and faithful, and we were marshalled off in regular staff style the services were two only, and the choir-nil, the whole carried out by the parson, his wife, myself, and the clerk. The congregation were mostly silent, or merely murmuring occasionally. The duty however was only arduous on Sundays."*

The beautiful Valency Valley ▼

Hardy was fond of Caddell Holder's geniality and his recounting of amusing stories, such as the time he was called to the bedside of a sickly man who said, after listening to a chapter from the Bible, that it had done him as much good as a glass of gin and water. Hardy's poem *Quid hic agis* is in part a reminiscence of a church service held by the Rev. Caddell Holder.

Also to be found on the wall at the west end of the nave, are copies of Hardy's drawings of the Saxon north door and of the bench ends which did not survive the restoration. The original pictures, which have been removed for safe keeping, were framed and donated to the church by Hardy in 1915.

Before leaving the church, it is worth considering a line from an article on St Juliot, written by A.L. Rowse in 1940... *"But proud as it must be of its visible memorials of its contact with one of the great English writers, it has still more reason to be proud of the intangible memories that cling to the place, the church, the porch, the stile, the hillside, the valley leading to the sea - that are indeed everywhere."*

Penventon
▼

Exit the churchyard by the southern stile and climb another style promptly on your right.

The fine views that confront you have changed little since Hardy and Emma walked down this very pathway. The fine isolated farmstead amid the sloping fields on the opposite side of the valley, is Halamiling, first recorded in 1327, spelt as Lamelyn, a Cornish name meaning 'mill valley'. In the 1870s, it was more of a hamlet than a farmstead as it consisted of four residences. The 62 acre farm was owned by Samuel Langford. He and his wife rented out part of the farmhouse and had three lodgers, all carpenters by trade. There were also two properties where their farm labourers and families resided and another building lodged two masons. Next to this settlement is Trafalgar built circa 1810-20.

It is a pastoral scene, very much as it was in Hardy's time. Sheep, beef and dairy cattle are farmed here along with crops of wheat, barley, oats, turnips, early potatoes and strawberries.

Once across three fields, cross over the path that descends from The Old Rectory and continue along a field hedge.

Here, according to a guide book dated 1901, stood *"a gigantic common laurel tree, the trunk of which measures 20 inches in diameter, and whose branches cover an area of 40 feet by 30."*

The ancient Medieval farmstead on your right is Penventon (Cornish: 'head of the spring') first recorded in 1300. It is, at the time of writing, a private residence. According to the census of 1871, the farmhouse with its 34 acres was owned by Richard Prout, who lived there with his mother and wife Jane. A grave in St Juliot's churchyard tells a tragic story of their three children, the first dying at the age of one in 1885, the second in 1892 at the age of 7 and the third in 1897 aged 21.

Go through the kissing-gate in the far corner of the field and enter the shaded woods that lead down the Valency Valley. Immediately to your left are the ruins of Penventon Cottage.

Surviving features of this 18th century building such as the cloam oven, window seat, storage spaces and fireplaces were doubtlessly in daily use when Hardy and Emma walked by. Then owned by a widower by the name of Joseph Lillacrapp, it was run as a market garden smallholding. A number of upright slate slabs in a small enclosure on the slopes above it are believed to be the remains of a raised granary. In 1891, it was unoccupied.

Continue down the path to the hamlet of Newmills.

In the 1800s this was a well trodden donkey track used by farmers travelling with their corn-laden carts down to the flour mill at Newmills. The Valency River once had several mills dotted along its banks, its fast flowing waters providing power for grinding the locally grown corn. It has even been suggested that the name Valency may be a corruption of the Cornish 'melin-jy', which means 'mill-house'.

Newmills hamlet is first recorded in 1628 and when Hardy and Emma walked past in the early 1870s, three families lived here. There was Samuel Bescombe, a farm labourer, with his wife Elizabeth, their two sons and two daughters. Thomas and Ann Baker with their son, lived at the smallholding of New Mills Farm and

▲ The ruins of Penventon Cottage

ran a boarding house which in 1871 had three lodgers.

Finally, there was the old miller himself, a widower by the name of Samuel Brokenshire. The first cottage you come across, nestled below amongst the trees on your left, is Elm Cottage dating from the mid 18th century. The next cluster of buildings is New Mills Cottage, also 18th century, which matches a description of the home of John Smith in Hardy's *A Pair of Blue Eyes*, as it once featured a chimney cloaked in ivy. Further on is Rose Cottage. Here, children were once brought for strawberry teas, where they could eat as much strawberries and cream as they liked for a shilling then, to cap the day, sports would be held in the valley fields below. Today some of the mill cottages are owned by the National Trust and are used as holiday lets.

Along this stretch of the Valency River was a little waterfall where, on Friday 19th August 1870, Thomas and Emma enjoyed a picnic of fruit and wine. Here they lost a glass tumbler and the occasion made a great impression on Hardy. Not only did he sketch the event, but wrote touchingly of the episode in two poems, *Under the Waterfall* and *Best Times*. He also describes a similar scene in *A Pair of Blue Eyes* *"... the river - such as it was - here pursued its course amid flagstones as level as a pavement, but divided by crevices of irregular width... They walked on together to a tiny cascade about a foot wide and high, and sat down beside it on flags that for nine months of the year were submerged beneath a gushing bourne. From their feet trickled the attenuated thread of water which alone remained to tell the intent and reason of this leaf-covered aisle, and journeyed on in a zigzag line till lost in the shade."*

▲
Rose Cottage, Newmills, circa 1890

Follow the stream all the way down to Boscastle village.

The lower end of the valley, the water-meadows and the car park area were changed dramatically by the flood event of 2004.

For the most part however, this lovely piece of Cornwall has changed little over the centuries and it is a pleasant thought that Thomas and Emma would have experienced much of this walk as you have done.

Valency River
circa 1890
▼

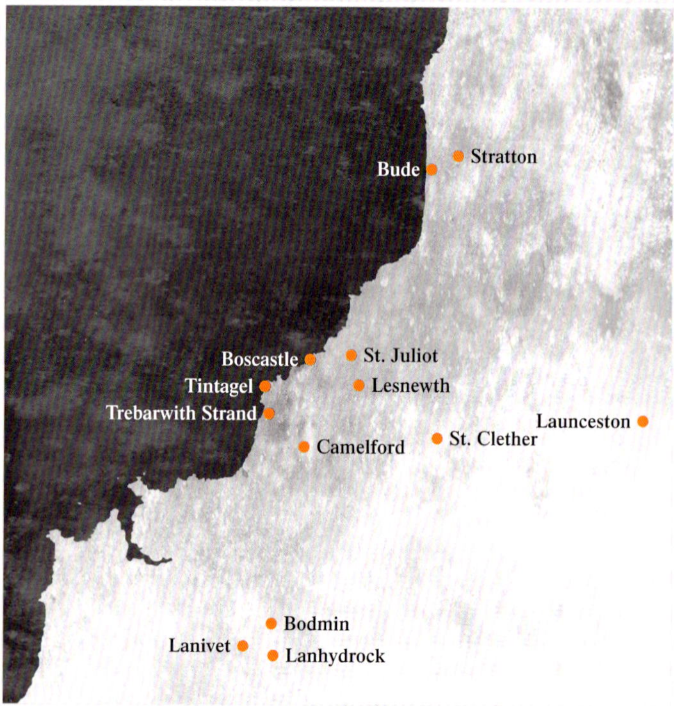
Stratton
Bude
Boscastle
St. Juliot
Tintagel
Lesnewth
Trebarwith Strand
Launceston
St. Clether
Camelford
Bodmin
Lanivet
Lanhydrock

Other Visits

Hardy, during his many visits to north Cornwall, toured the beauty spots of the district with Emma, sometimes walking alongside her as she rode her mare, Fanny. At other times they went by chaise and were accompanied on occasion by the Rev. Holder and his wife. Many of the locations were eventually incorporated in his writings, especially in the novel *A Pair of Blue Eyes*.

The sites of special note are listed overleaf, in alphabetical order.

St Benet's Abbey, Lanivet

It was here that Emma stayed during the autumn and winter of 1865-66, having suffered exhaustion after nursing her sister Helen who had been injured in a road accident near Launceston. The Abbey at that time was owned by Capt. Charles Serjeant and his wife Jane, friends of the Gifford family. The house had been bequeathed to Jane by the previous owner, an eccentric rector by the name of Rev. William Phillips Flamank, described by Emma as *"An invalid with a spinal complaint"* who *"...lived in his bed, boarded-up on three sides."* She goes on to say *"...quarrelled with all his relatives."* and *"possessed a remarkable power of winning in any lottery."*

▲ St Benet's Abbey, circa 1900

The original building was constructed in the 15th century by the Benedictine Order as a Lazar House, to quarantine lepers. Later in its history it was rented

Reperry Cross
▼

from Bodmin Friary by the Giffard family, who built a chapel here, of which the tower remains. The Chapel of St Benedict was first mentioned when it was licensed to celebrate Divine Service in 1411. By the mid 19th century it was described by one chronicler as being *"mutilated and spoilt"* by the owner. Today it is a guest house with a reputation as being one of the most haunted in the British Isles. Perhaps Emma experienced this, as she wrote of it having *"an old-time sadness"* and *"One's soul was not refreshed out of doors, where we were amongst the bones of the former immured people, though no cemetery could be seen or known."*

Hardy is thought to have stayed here during August 1872, having sailed down from London to Plymouth on the packet boat, the 'Avoca'. His intention was to visit the Gifford family at nearby Kirland Manor and announce his proposal to marry Emma.

From here, Emma and Hardy roamed around the countryside, as described in his poem *Near Lanivet, 1872*, a piece that captures a sense of foreboding and in hindsight, the tragic vision of things to come. Returning home after a day's walk Hardy writes how they stopped to rest near a *"stunted handpost"*, thought by some to be the one at nearby Reperry Cross.

It was also from here that he made excursions to past haunts like Tintagel and St Juliot, where he met amongst other visitors there, a Miss d'Arville *"...a delightful old lady from Bath, who had a canary that fainted and fell to the bottom of the cage whenever a cat came into the room, or the picture of a cat was shown it."*

Bodmin

Called Rou'tor Town by Hardy, it was here that the Gifford family moved in 1860 after financial difficulties forced them from their Plymouth home. Their first residence was at a house in Tower Hill, situated opposite the ancient Tower Hill Farm where Perkin Warbeck is said to have crowned himself King. Emma's Place as it is known today, was described in her memoirs as *"...close to the Church and practically in the churchyard, the larder looking into it and below the level, therefore quite unfit for food."* Emma did not take to the place and thought Bodmin *"a town that never enlarged itself."* The family stayed here only a few months, moving on to Kirland Manor, which is situated on the outskirts of the town. Surrounded by a rookery, an orchard and garden which pleased her father immensely, as he was a keen amateur gardener, it had

▲ Fore Street, Bodmin circa 1890

its own bathing pool and a stream full of fish.

During the 19th century, Bodmin established itself as the county's administrative centre. It was a time of expansion and development, with the County Asylum completed in 1820 and the town's large gaol becoming the County Gaol in 1829. By 1838 Bodmin had become became the sole location for the Cornish Assizes, where criminal and civil trials were held bi-annually in the Shire Hall. Because of this, Bodmin gained a grim reputation; as one Assize Judge commented, it was *"Out of the world and into Bodmin"*, and an old saying went that there were two ways to the town *"Taken or put to Bodmin."*

Shire Hall, Mount Folly, Bodmin circa 1875

CAMELFORD

The small market town on the edge of Bodmin Moor, was an important coaching station in the mid 19th century, being situated on the main route from London to Falmouth. It was then notable for not possessing a parish church, the closest being at Lanteglos nearby.

Tennyson, in his Arthurian quest, visited the town twice as it had a reputation for being the site of King Arthur's fatal last battle of Camlan. Nearby, at Slaughterbridge, an inscribed stone rests on the bank of the River Camel, and it was here that Tennyson, following his Arthurian trail, fell into the stream and subsequently returned to his lodgings in the town, laughing.

Named Camelton in the novel *A Pair Of Blue Eyes*, it was where a new railway station had been opened and Elfride's coffin was taken from the train to an awaiting hearse. In actual fact, the Camelford railway station did not open until 1893, many years after the novel's first publication. With its arrival, easier access was to be had to the remote villages and harbours of the district, thus spelling an end to the flourishing trade of ports such as Boscastle and Port Isaac. Hardy himself waited here for a coach to take him to Boscastle in 1913.

The station, like many others in Cornwall, suffered the axe of the Beeching Act and was closed in 1966.

Camelford circa 1900 ▼

ST CLETHER

On an evening in May 1871, Hardy and Emma drove here by pony and chaise and visited the vicarage, where they enquired after the curate's son, William Serjeant who was suffering from consumption. This visit is the subject of the poem *The Face At The Casement*. The young man who watched them drive away that evening, died a year later at the age of 23 and his tomb can be seen in the south east corner of the churchyard opposite.

St Clether boasts an association with another Victorian writer Rev. Sabine Baring-Gould, author of the novel *In The Roar Of The Sea* and the hymn *Onwards Christian Soldier*. It was he who restored the Holy Well Chapel, which was the parish church prior to the Norman invasion. Like other ecclesiastical buildings in the area, it had fallen into disrepair by the 19th century with its walls and roof in ruins. The Holy Well Chapel (the largest in Cornwall), was re-dedicated in 1900 and stands next to the Well itself. The Norman church was almost totally destroyed by fire in 1865 but its impressive tower, dating from 1420, survived along with two bells.

▲ The grave of William Serjeant in St Clether's churchyard

St Clether's Old Rectory ▼

LANHYDROCK

Lanhydrock House, prior to the fire of 1881
▼

Situated a few miles south of Bodmin, the house, now owned by the National Trust, has its fifty rooms open to the public. It is surrounded by wooded parkland and Victorian gardens, famous for their spectacular spring displays of rhododendrons, magnolias and camellias.

The name is Cornish, meaning a monastic Barton, and the land had for a long time been a possession of the priory of St Petroc in Bodmin, but during the 16th century the Robartes family gained ownership of the property having made their fortune in the tin trade. When Hardy visited, the estate was in the hands of Thomas James Agar-Robartes who had been created Baron Robartes of Lanhydrock and Truro in 1869.

On the 4th April 1881, a disastrous fire destroyed the house, leaving only the north wing, the entrance porch and gatehouse. Lady Robartes, aged 68, died a few days later from shock. Lord Robartes, who never got over this loss, died the following year. Their son, Thomas Charles Robartes, succeeded as the 2nd Baron Robartes and it was he who undertook the reconstruction of Lanhydrock, using the same grey granite and preserving the original design.

Endelstow House, in *A Pair Of Blue Eyes*, is purported to be largely based on this property.

LESNEWTH

Once the capital of a sub-division in the Old Hundred of Trigg, a church has existed here since Saxon times. This building however was burnt and pillaged by marauding Danes, leaving a desolate site on which the Normans later built their church. As in the case of St Juliot, Lesnewth's St Michaels & All Angels, was by the mid 18th century in a dilapidated state and in 1862 the architect J.P. St Aubyn was called in to restore it. St Aubyn had little of the sympathy for conservation that Hardy possessed and dynamite was used to demolish parts of the building. Little of its Norman structure remains today and of its particularly fine roofs and carved woodwork, nothing survives.

It was here that on Sunday 14th August 1870, Hardy attended evensong with Emma and a young churchwarden lit candles for the service. The poem *The Young Churchwarden* was based on this encounter.

The monumental wheel-headed wayside cross that stands in the churchyard was erected here in 1872 after being rescued from a nearby farm where attempts had been made to carve out one side and use it as a pig trough.

▲
St Michaels & All Angels Church, Lesnewth

Launceston

Launceston Station circa 1890
▼

Once known as Dunheved, Launceston was the capital of Cornwall until 1838. This ancient town guarded the gateway to the Duchy in Medieval times and its Norman walls and castle continue to stand proud, overlooking the expanse of Dartmoor and the Tamar Valley. Described by Betjeman as *"the most interesting inland town in Cornwall"* its elegant Georgian houses still line the narrow thoroughfares and market square.

Here, Hardy's epic twelve hour train journey from Dorchester on the 7th of March 1870, finally came to its end at 4.03pm. There had been eight station stops en-route from Plymouth alone, taking one and a half hours to complete. Interested parties can still experience the flavour of such journeys, as the steam locomotives of the Launceston Steam Railway haul open and closed carriages through the Kensey Valley throughout the summer.

Climbing the steep hill from the station to the town, Hardy went in search of refreshment and a coach to take him to Boscastle. This would not have been the regular coach service between Launceston and Boscastle, which was provided by John French, every Tuesday.

Launceston in the 19th century had no shortage of watering holes. At least fifteen inns existed along with several cider and beer houses known as 'kiddleywinks' plus two hotels, namely the King's

Arms and the White Hart. Hardy probably chose the latter to imbibe in. Situated in the market square, the White Hart Hotel is still predominant, with its grand Georgian features and Norman doorway (believed to have been removed from the Castle's chapel).

Emma had a strong connection with the town, as her much-loved uncle, aunts and cousins lived here. In her *Recollections*, she writes of the happy times she spent with them...

"We stayed over Christmas, and had good cheer, the Xmas waits, parties, and the usual festivities of the season, - and many visits to the grand old castle and walks in the neighbourhood we had."

Hardy visited the town on several occasions between the years of 1870-74, and 43 years later, he returned to walk its streets again in an effort to recapture those nostalgic days. He subsequently wrote the poem *St Launce's Revisited*. Calling at the inn once again, he pondered on the ghostly encounters that he was about to face before embarking for Boscastle. On this occasion the branchline to Camelford was in operation and was a more convenient stop, whilst his first journey from Launceston to St Juliot was in Hardy's description, a *"dreary yet poetical drive."* Sixteen miles in all, it crossed the open ground that skirts the moor to Hallworthy, then onwards past Otterham to Tresparrett Posts, descending then to Hennett and eventually up the narrow lane to St Juliot.

These place names are found incorporated in his poem *A Man Was Drawing Near to Me*

Launceston, originally named St Kirrs in his 1873 publication of *A Pair Of Blue Eyes*, was later changed to St Launce's; it was the market town and station nearest to Endelstow.

▲
Launceston's White Hart Hotel 1894

Launceston's Southgate 1890
▼

The Falcon Hotel, where Elfride prepares for her journey to London, is most probably the White Hart.

No. 20 Church Street with its 'barley twist' cast iron columns and decorated friezes is thought to be where the vendor of *"flutes, and fiddles, and grand pianners"* plied his trade.

STRATTON & BUDE

Emma and Hardy visited the area, travelling by pony and trap along the undulating coastal lane that winds its way from Boscastle, past the Strangles, Crackington Haven and Millook, to Bude.

Up until the early 19th century Bude was only a handful of cottages and fish cellars overshadowed by the ancient market town of Stratton. But with the onset of the Victorian era, with its obsession for healthy sea air and bathing, the town gradually grew to become a most fashionable watering place.

In 1847, Tennyson holidayed here and it is said that in his enthusiasm to glimpse the sea he promptly fell over a garden wall and broke his leg, consequently transforming his salubrious vacation to a convalescence at the Falcon Hotel.

Named Stratleigh in the novel *A Pair of Blue Eyes*, it is where Mr Swancourt marries Mrs Troyton.

▲ Bude Canal and The Falcon Hotel circa 1860

TINTAGEL

Known as Trevena in 1870, the village was then a very remote place where, as Emma recalled *"strange old-fashioned people with old-world ways lived in sheltered niches on the high ground."* The village was then beginning to experience the influx of tourism, having been put firmly on the map by Tennyson's *Morte d'Arthur* (1842) and *Idylls of the King* (1859). Charles Dickens, Wilkie Collins, Algernon Swinburne - a great favourite of Hardy's, had all passed through on their itinerary of Cornwall.

A few days previous Hardy's visit, clergyman, diarist Francis Kilvert took a guided tour of the island, bought photographs and dined at an inn, in the archetypal fashion of a present day tourist. Hardy and Emma made the same circuit but somehow found themselves locked within the gated walls of the 12th century castle, waving a handkerchief to alert the key holder to their plight.

▲
Trevena as it was then known, circa 1900

Tintagel Haven
and Castle,
circa 1875
▼

Emma knew the area well already. Her sister Helen had lived here as an employed companion to an eccentric old lady named Miss Robartes. Emma stayed here briefly recuperating from an illness and when she returned home, the elderly hostess sent a pony as a gift, Emma's much loved brown mare, named Fanny.

Emma's own unpublished novel *The Maid on the Shore* was set on this coast and in her *Recollections* she wrote... *"In the winter the storms were magnificent and the wind dangerous to contend with on the cliffs. I was nearly blown into the Atlantic ocean and clung to the rocks frightened."* The incident inspired Hardy and is recounted in *A Pair of Blue Eyes*.

In 1923, Hardy completed his poetic play for mummers *The Famous Tragedy of the Queen of Cornwall at Tintagel in Lyonnesse*, first conceived during his 1870 visit. He wrote afterwards... *"I visited the place 44 years ago with an Iseult of my own, and of course she was mixed in the vision of the other."* It was his last look back at Cornwall with all its tragic connotations. His pen and ink drawing of how he imagined the castle once to have been, adorned the cover.

St Materiana Church, Tintagel, at the time of Hardy's last visit
▼

Although Tintagel, by name and by nature, has altered greatly since Hardy's time, there are some significant buildings that haven't, for example the Old Post Office and also Tintagel's wonderful church. St Materiana is one of Cornwall's least spoiled churches and has changed little since the days of the Norman Earls who built the castle. Emma painted a charming watercolour of the church interior as a momento; but for Hardy it was made memorable by a later, upsetting incident. On Sunday the 10th of September 1916, while attending a service with his second wife Florence, the couple were moved from their pew to make way for the choir. Hardy took offence at this gesture, and consequently walked out in the middle of the sermon. *"It was saddening enough"* he wrote later *"..that we were inhospitably received in a church so much visited and appreciated by one (Emma) we both had known so well."*

He never visited the area again, thus closing an epoch that had begun with so much enchantment.

TREBARWITH STRAND

Emma recalled a *"dawdling, enjoyable"* visit with Hardy here in August 1870 *"where donkeys were onerously employed to get seaweed for the farmers."* This was common practice along the shores of north Cornwall and the seaweed was used to fertilise the fields. Sand was also carried away to nearby farms, where it was mixed with turf, weeds and some farmyard manure to form a good top dressing for the soil. Granny and Granfer Lobb were a well photographed local couple who toiled with their donkeys here.

The slate quarries that surround the beach, both inland and along the cliffs, have been in existence since Medieval times and it was at nearby Penpethy Quarry, that Hardy came on the 9th of March 1870 to select roofing slates for St Juliot Church. This visit is reflected in his poem *Green Slates*. The beach and surrounding coastline remains unchanged since Emma painted her watercolours here, though what is now the Port William pub, was in their time a row of coastguard cottages.

Named Barwith Strand in the novel *A Pair of Blue Eyes*, it is where the picnic party took place and the little cottage mentioned is probably Surf Cottage.

▲ Trebarwith Strand circa 1870

▲
Pentargon

THE ROUTE

The following pages summarise the directions of the walk that explores the haunts of Thomas and Emma Hardy.

The map sections are based on the Ordnance Survey, dated 1883. In places, hedges have now been removed and some places mentioned in the text may not be shown.

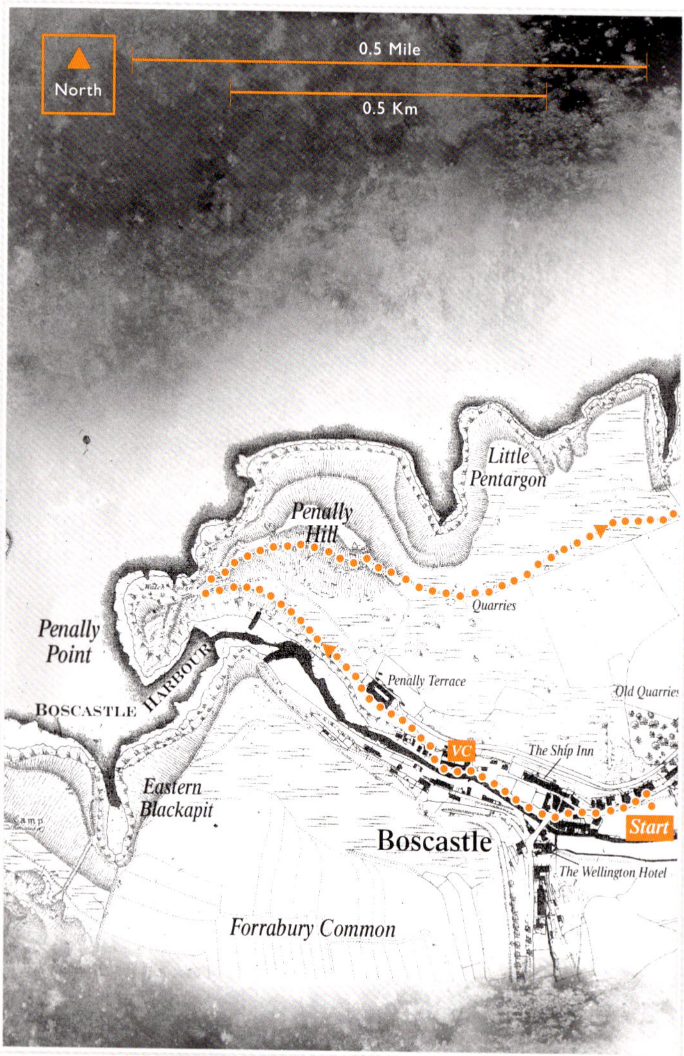
North
0.5 Mile
0.5 Km
Little Pentargon
Penally Hill
Quarries
Penally Point
BOSCASTLE HARBOUR
Penally Terrace
Old Quarries
VC
The Ship Inn
Eastern Blackapit
Start
Boscastle
The Wellington Hotel
Forrabury Common

Starting from the car park, head down towards the harbour.

When you reach the road bridge, cross over the road and follow the lane that runs along the north bank of the river.

Beyond the Visitor Centre and the new bridge that spans the Valency, bear right and carry on up to Penally Terrace.

From Penally Terrace, a path leads up along the north side of the harbour. On the ascent to the flagpole at the top of Penally Hill (288 ft), there is, looking south, an excellent view of the harbour.

From Penally Hill walk along the coastal footpath heading north towards Pentargon following hedges of weathered and lichen-covered stones.

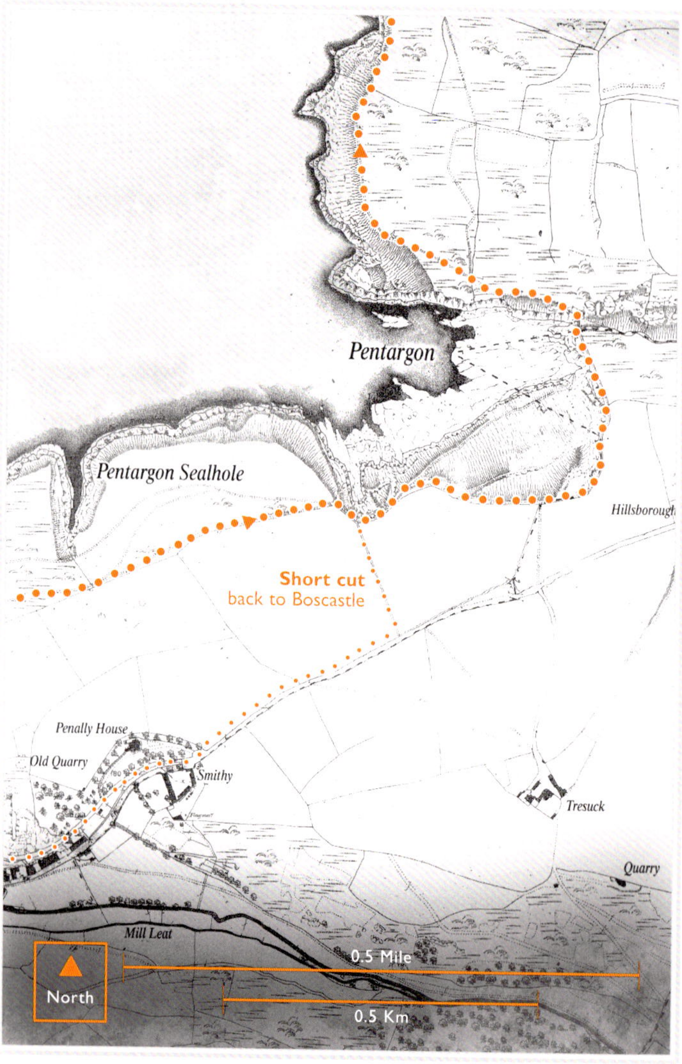
Pentargon
Pentargon Sealhole
Hillsborough
Short cut
back to Boscastle
Penally House
Old Quarry
Smithy
Tresuck
Quarry
Mill Leat
North
0.5 Mile
0.5 Km

Short-cut...

From above Pentargon Cove, one can return to Boscastle by taking a path across the fields towards the Bude road (B3263). To avoid the traffic, use the footpath that runs parallel to the road and then continue along the Green Cut path, back into the village - a round trip of about two and a half miles.

To continue on the long route...

Leave Pentargon and its waterfall behind, climb the winding footpath to the top of the next headland and then descend the steep-sided valley out to Beeny Cliff itself.

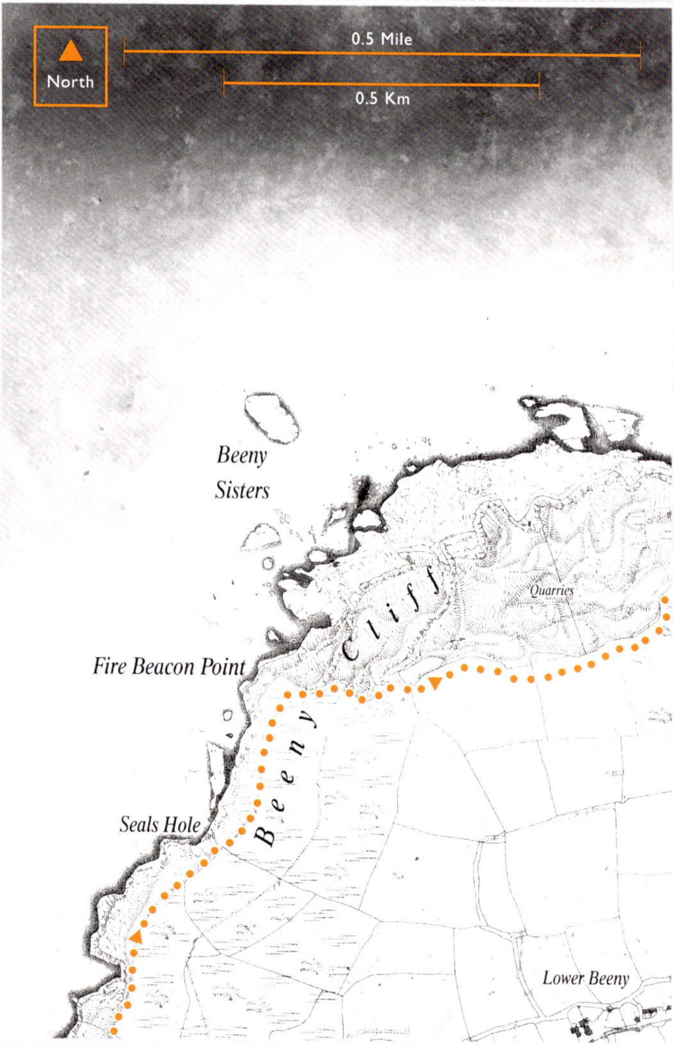

North
0.5 Mile
0.5 Km
Beeny Sisters
Quarries
Beeny Cliff
Fire Beacon Point
Seals Hole
Lower Beeny

From Beeny, the coast path climbs to Fire Beacon Point. There is now an easier inland route which avoids some of the steeper sections. Both ways join again just before Firebeacon Point.

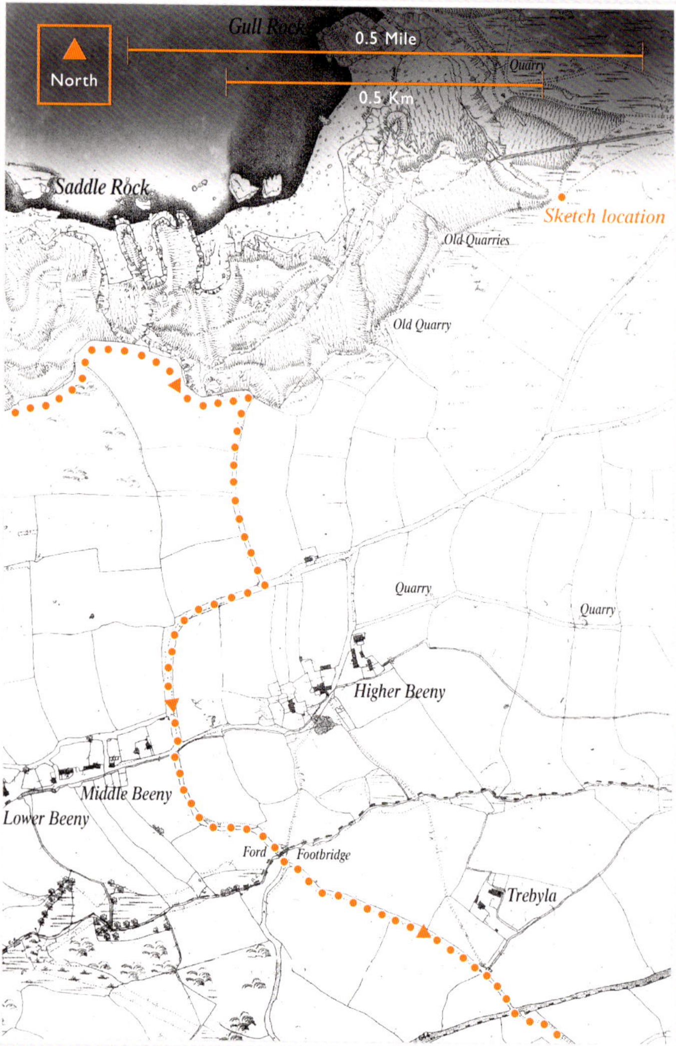
North
0.5 Mile
0.5 Km
Gull Rock
Quarry
Saddle Rock
Sketch location
Old Quarries
Old Quarry
Quarry
Quarry
Higher Beeny
Middle Beeny
Lower Beeny
Ford
Footbridge
Trebyla

Strike inland along the path at the end of the third field from Fire Beacon Point. (Should you wish to stand at the exact spot where Hardy sketched his Beeny Cliff, then follow the coastpath onwards for some 250 yards.)

To retrace the steps of Emma and Hardy returning to St Juliot, follow the hedge. It will lead you out past North Lodge onto a metalled road, here turn right and follow the lane around a bend, downwards into the valley, passing the 18th century farmstead of Middle Beeny and the 16th century farmhouse of Lower Beeny on your right. Once you reach the valley, ignore the first marked footpath on your left, cross over a culvert and a few yards ahead, follow the track up to a gate; to the left is a wooden stile. Proceed ahead, across a field and along the farm track of Trebyla, then out onto the main Boscastle to Bude road (B3263).

Tremorle
The Old School
The Old Rectory
Old Quarry
Penventon
North
0.5 Mile
0.5 Km

Carefully cross the road and climb the stile directly in front, then veer 11 o'clock and follow the path across the field and on towards St Juliot. This path crosses five fields in all, over some ancient stiles, and eventually emerges through a gate opposite Penventon Farm. To your left, you can find the old Parish School, now converted into a private residence.

(Should you wish to see the Old Rectory of St Juliot, to which Thomas Hardy came in March 1870, then turn immediately right and drop down the drive.)

Resuming the walk from the gate opposite Penventon Farm, join the road and bear right, following it for some half a mile to reach St Juliot Church.

Tremorle
The Old School
The Old Rectory
Old Quarry
Penventon
St Juliot Church
Trafalgar
Allemelon
(Halamiling)
North
0.5 Mile
0.5 Km

After visiting the church, exit the churchyard by the southern stile and climb another style promptly on your right.

Once across three fields you cross over the path that descends from The Old Rectory.

Continue along the hedge of the fourth field, passing the old farmstead of Penventon.

Go through the kissing-gate in the far corner of the field and enter the shaded woods that lead down the Valency Valley. Immediately to your left there stands the ruin of Penventon Cottage.

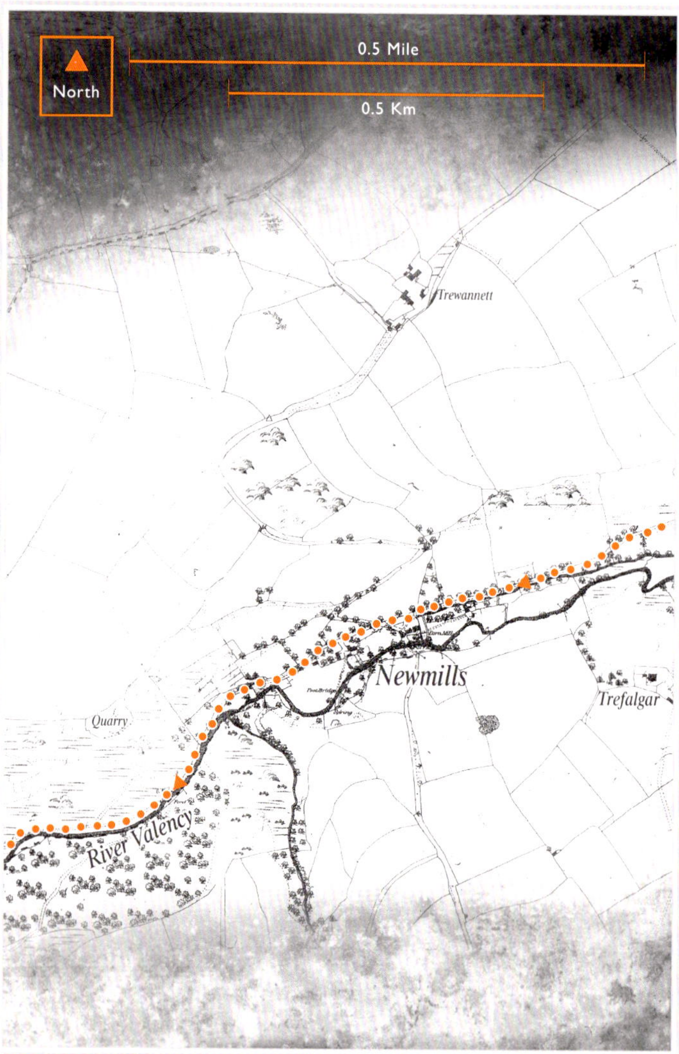
North
0.5 Mile
0.5 Km
Trewannett
Newmills
Trefalgar
Quarry
River Valency

Continue along the pathway down to the secluded hamlet of Newmills, and then onwards, following the course of the stream.

0.5 Mile
North
Pentargon
0.5 Km
le
Hillsborough
Tresuck
Quarry
MINSTER WOODS

Keep ahead through the wooded valley with the Valency River and Minster Woods on your left.

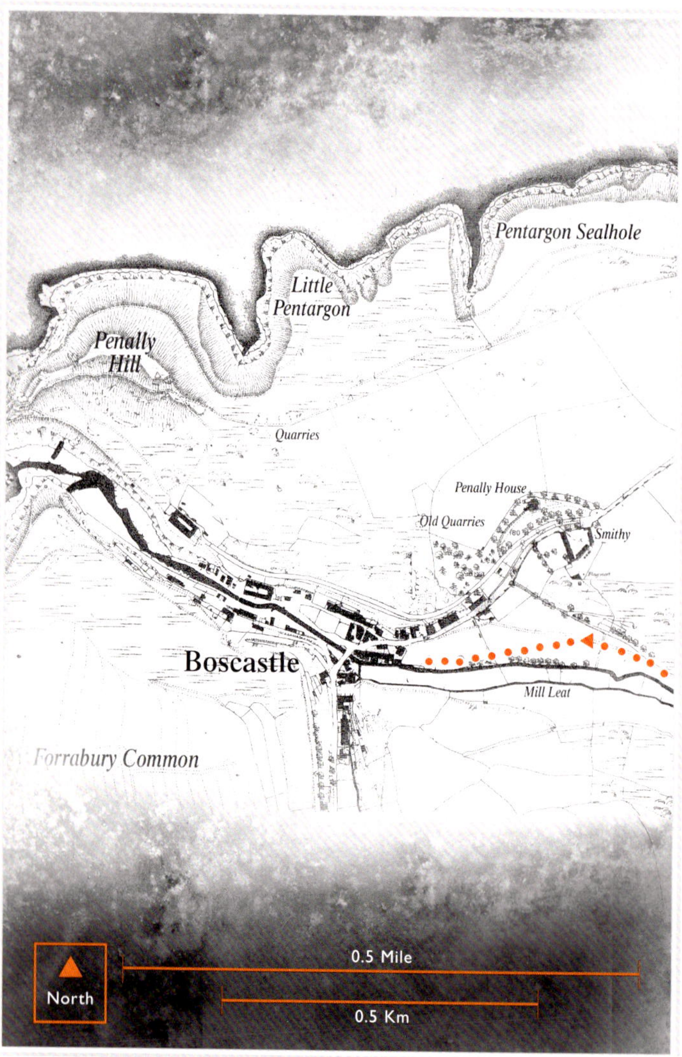
Pentargon Sealhole
Little
Pentargon
Penally
Hill
Quarries
Penally House
Old Quarries
Smithy
Boscastle
Mill Leat
Forrabury Common
0.5 Mile
North
0.5 Km

The path soon emerges into more open ground and eventually leads back to Boscastle, your journey's end.

Bibliography

The Complete Poems of Thomas Hardy. Edited by James Gibson. Macmillan, 1976.

Hardy's Love Poems. Edited with notes and an introduction by Carl J. Weber. Macmillan, 1963.

A Pair of Blue Eyes. Thomas Hardy. Oxford University Press, 2005.

The Famous Tragedy of the Queen of Cornwall at Tintagel in Lyonnesse. Thomas Hardy. Macmillan, 1923.

Personal Writings. Thomas Hardy. Macmillan, 1967.

The Personal Notebooks of Thomas Hardy. Thomas Hardy. Macmillan, 1978.

The Collected Letters of Thomas Hardy. Vol.1 : 1840-1892. Edited by Richard Little Purdy and Michael Millgate. Clarendon Press, 1978.

Dearest Emmie: Thomas Hardy's Letters to His First Wife. Edited by Carl J. Webber. Macmillan, 1963.

The Life of Thomas Hardy 1840 -1928. F.E. Hardy. Macmillan, 1962.

Young Thomas Hardy. Robert Gittings. Heinemann Educational, 1975.

Concerning Thomas Hardy : A Composite Portrait from Memory. Edited by D.F.B. Skilton, 1968.

The Domestic Life of Thomas Hardy 1921-1928. Ellen E. Titterington. Toucan Press, 1963

Thomas Hardy : An Illustrated Biography. Timothy O'Sullivan. Macmillan, 1975.

Thomas Hardy : A Pictorial Guide. Hugh Brasnett. Lodge Copse, 1990.

Thomas Hardy: A Biography. Michael Millgate. Oxford University Press, 1982.

Some Recollections by Emma Hardy. Revised Edition, Oxford University Press, 1979.

Emma Hardy Diaries. Edited by Richard H. Taylor. Mid Northumberland Arts Group, 1985.

The Country of 'A Pair of Blue Eyes'. M.A. Winchcombe. Third edition, revised by Charles P.C. Pettit, Thomas Hardy Society, 2000.

The Wormwood Cup. Kenneth Phelps. Lodenek Press, 1975.

The First Mrs Thomas Hardy. Denys Kay-Robinson. Macmillan, 1979.

A Hardy Companion : A Guide to the Works of Thomas Hardy and their Background. F. B. Pinion. - Macmillan, 1968.

The Hardy Guides : A Guide to the West Country. Hermann Lea. Edited by Gregory Stevens Cox. Vol.2. Penguin, 1986.

Hardy Landscapes. Gordon Beningfield. Viking, 1990.

The Landscape of Thomas Hardy. Denys Kay-Robinson. Webb & Bower, 1984.

St Juliot Church and Thomas Hardy. Charles P.C. Pettit. Thomas Hardy Society, 1986.

Thomas Hardy and Rural England. Merryn Williams. Macmillan, 1972.

Thomas Hardy's England. John Fowles & Jo Draper. Bloomsbury, 1989.

Visitors to Cornwall. Ida Procter. Dyllansow Truran, 1982.

A Mere Interlude : Some Literary Visitors in Lyonnesse. Patten, 1992.

Kilvert's Cornish Diary. Francis Kilvert. Edited by Richard Maber & Angela Tregoning. Alison Hodge, 1989.

Sundays In Cornwall. The Bells of Bottreaux. R.S. Hawker. Thomas Guthrie, 1864.

Footprints of Former Men In Far Cornwall. R.S. Hawker. Westaway Books, 1948.

Sabine Baring-Gould, Squarson, Writer and Folklorist, 1834-1924. Bickford Holland Cohan Dickinson. David & Charles, 1970.

Tour in Cornwall and the Scilly Isles. Alfred Tennyson. Macmillan, 1897.

Deanery of Trigg Minor. Sir John Maclean. 1873.

Memories of Boscastle & Tintagel. The Cornish & Devon Post.

Boscastle. Michael Williams. Bossiney Books, 1978.

Boscastle. The National Trust, 1986.

A Brief History of Boscastle. Rod & Anne Knight. 1999.

In the Footsteps of Thomas & Emma Hardy.

Written by Heulyn & Ginny Lewis.

Design, photography & artwork by Heulyn Lewis.

First published by NCDC 2003

Published by Pelican Studio - Trenant Point - Looe - Cornwall - PL13 2AA

Special thanks to:

The National Trust at the Boscastle Visitor Centre for their assistance with the production of this edition.

Charles P. C. Pettit for his invaluable contribution.

Sally Searle, The Old Rectory, St Juliot for her great help with this project.

Archive photographs reproduced by kind permission of:

The Cornwall Centre - Redruth; Dorset County Museum - Dorchester.

Private collectors, including Mike Webber and Colin Brewer.

W. Gibbons' painting of Boscastle 1875 reproduced by kind permission of the owner, Mike Mills.

This book can be ordered direct from the publisher
email: pelicanstudioinfo@gmail.com

Printed on recyclable paper made from wood grown in sustainably managed forests.

ISBN 978-0-9572340-1-7